MONSOON TALES

MONSOON TALES

through the lens of my 9th floor in Bangalore

Shruti Sharma

An Ink Gladiators Press® Publication

Ink Gladiators Press®
Publishing and promoting warriors on life's battlefield

Ink Gladiators Press is an ePublishing company whose mission is to publish and promote writers, poets, lyricists, artists and photographers through our current worldwide market distribution of over 3 billion readership. It is not affiliated with any other organization and is an independent ePublishing house. For Earthians who want to publish with us, check out our ongoing publishing opportunities at Our Earthians Community Group, or write to us to learn more about our high-end professional Celestial Sky Services at the following email address: contact@inkgladiatorspress.com.

First Edition

Monsoon Tales: through the lens of my 9th floor in Bangalore

Ink Gladiators Press®
Printed in Bangalore 560077, India
www.inkgladiatorspress.com
ISBN: 978-93-90766-09-3

Credits:
Cover Photography – Shruti Sharma
Cover and Interior Design – Leonie Belle Hawk
Editor – Reena Doss

For Mom, Dad, Akshay and Surbhi,
a loving family is my greatest gift

Author's Note

Dear Readers,

To put it bluntly, this book was unexpected.

It all started one Monsoon evening (in 2020) when I happened to step out onto my 9th floor balcony at just the right time to catch a spectacular sunset. Despite having stayed in this flat for years, I somehow never managed to look toward that narrow window where the sun bids goodbye or prop my feet up and watch as a storm played out in all its elemental glory. I just never seemed to have the time. There was always something to do, somewhere to be, some screen holding all my attention.

If not for the lockdown, I daresay I wouldn't have slowed down long enough to notice. Now, every evening, I find myself, phone in hand, hanging outside more and more. Who would have known that being forced to stay inside would actually lead me to discover the wealth of beauty that had been patiently waiting for me all these years to take notice.

However, here I am with over a thousand photographs taken during this quarantine period. It was difficult to select my favourites but these 36 captures that I finally chose along with my words are a testament to the fact that the best of things often originate from the worst of circumstances.

Through Monsoon Tales, I've tried to document the moments that brought me so much joy amidst this rather uncertain year of trials. I hope they do the same for you.

Thank you for joining me on this journey.

Best wishes,

@shrutiscapes

Table Of Contents

this monsoon came marching
over a city in hiding...

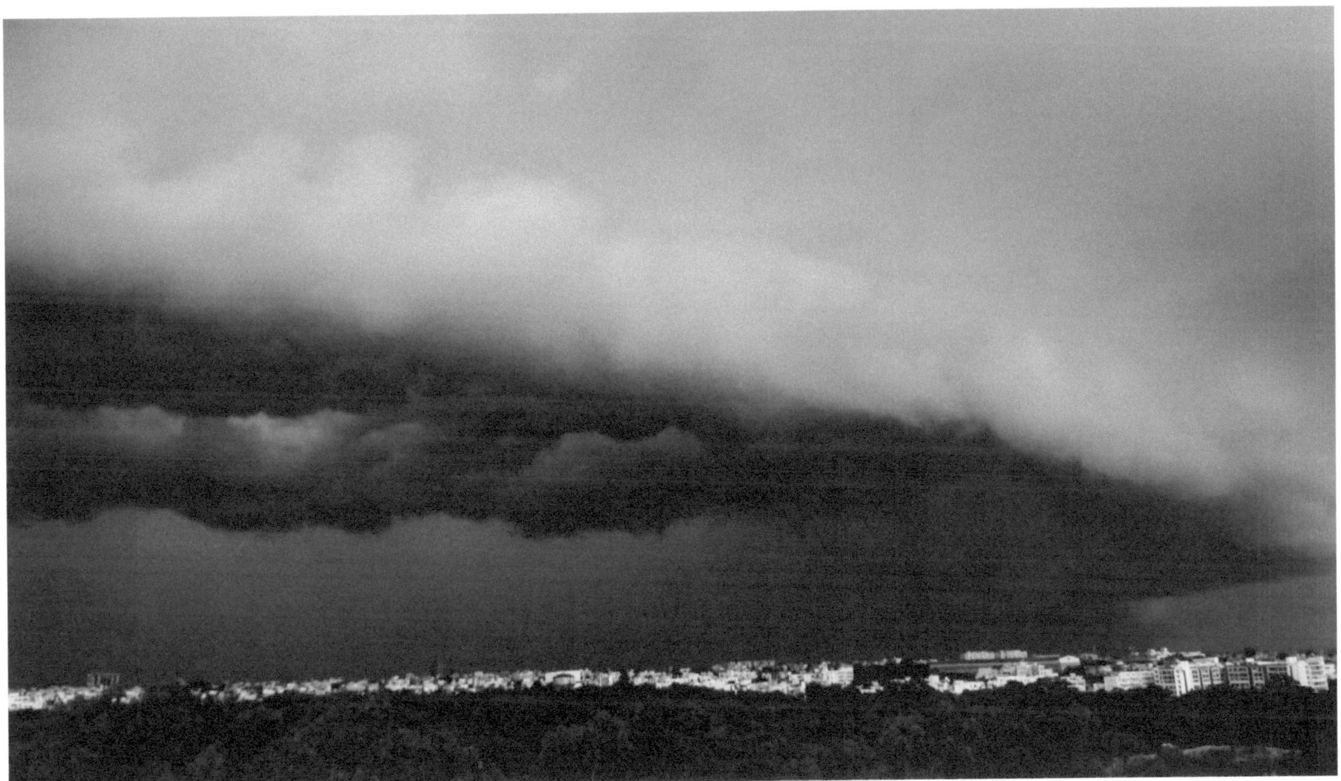

the skies raged
as we finally understood
the meaning of a cage

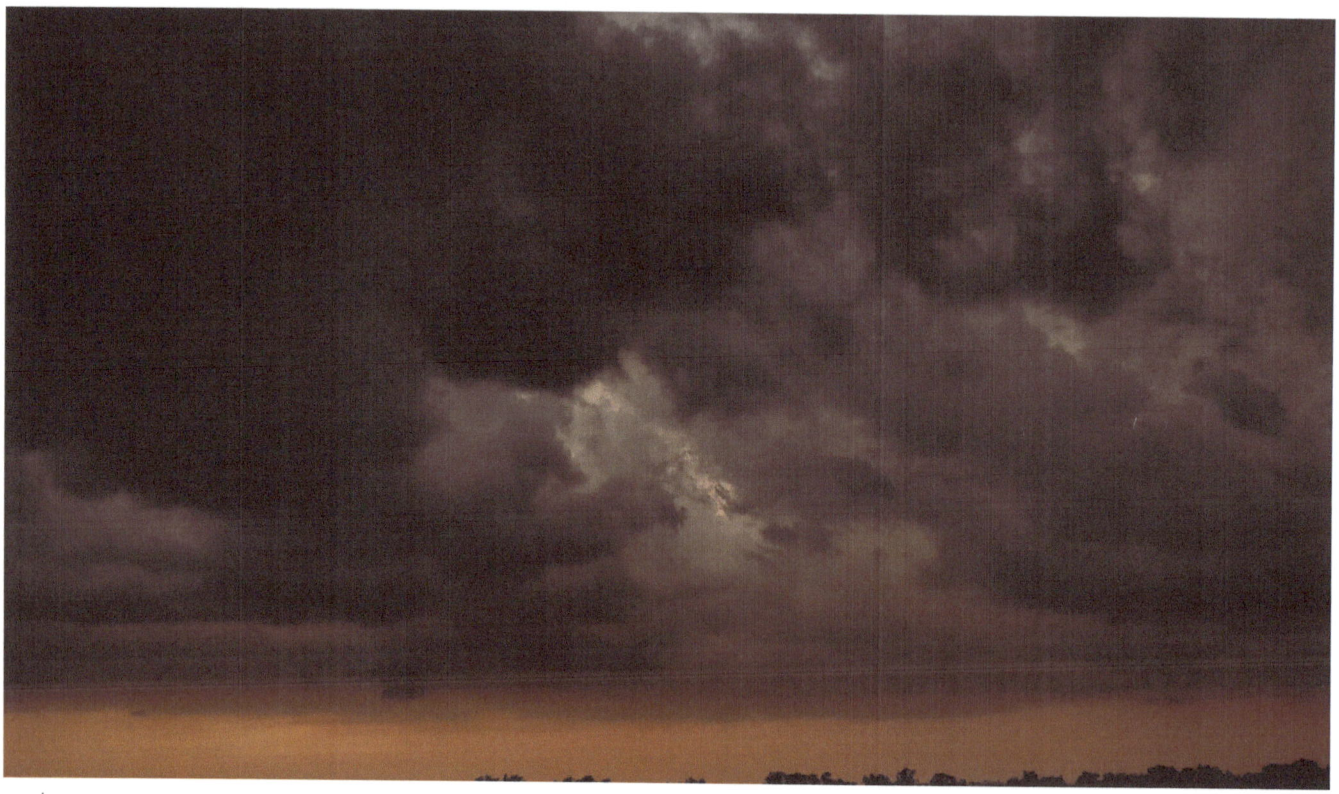

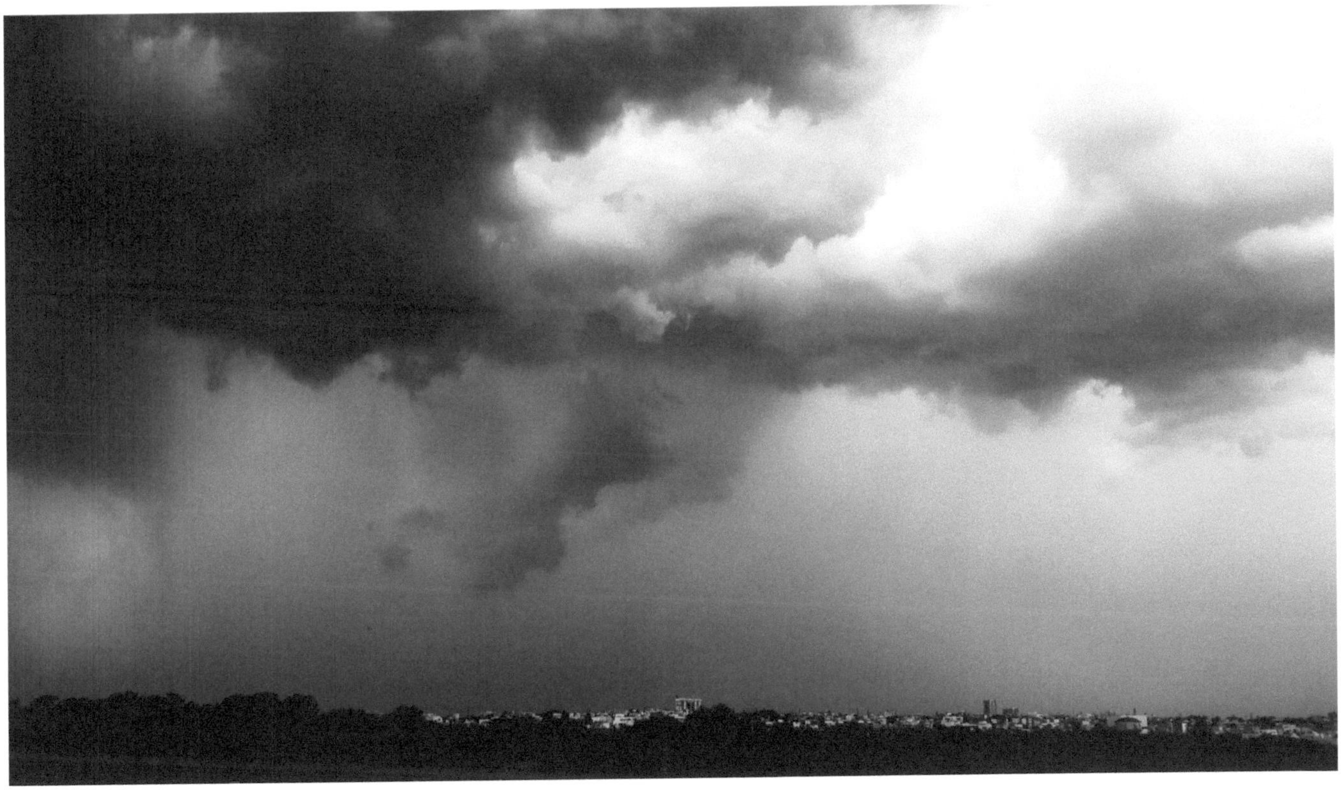

the most atavistic of seasons
the wild whispers in its winds
the most uncivilised of seasons
the air brews thundering chaos

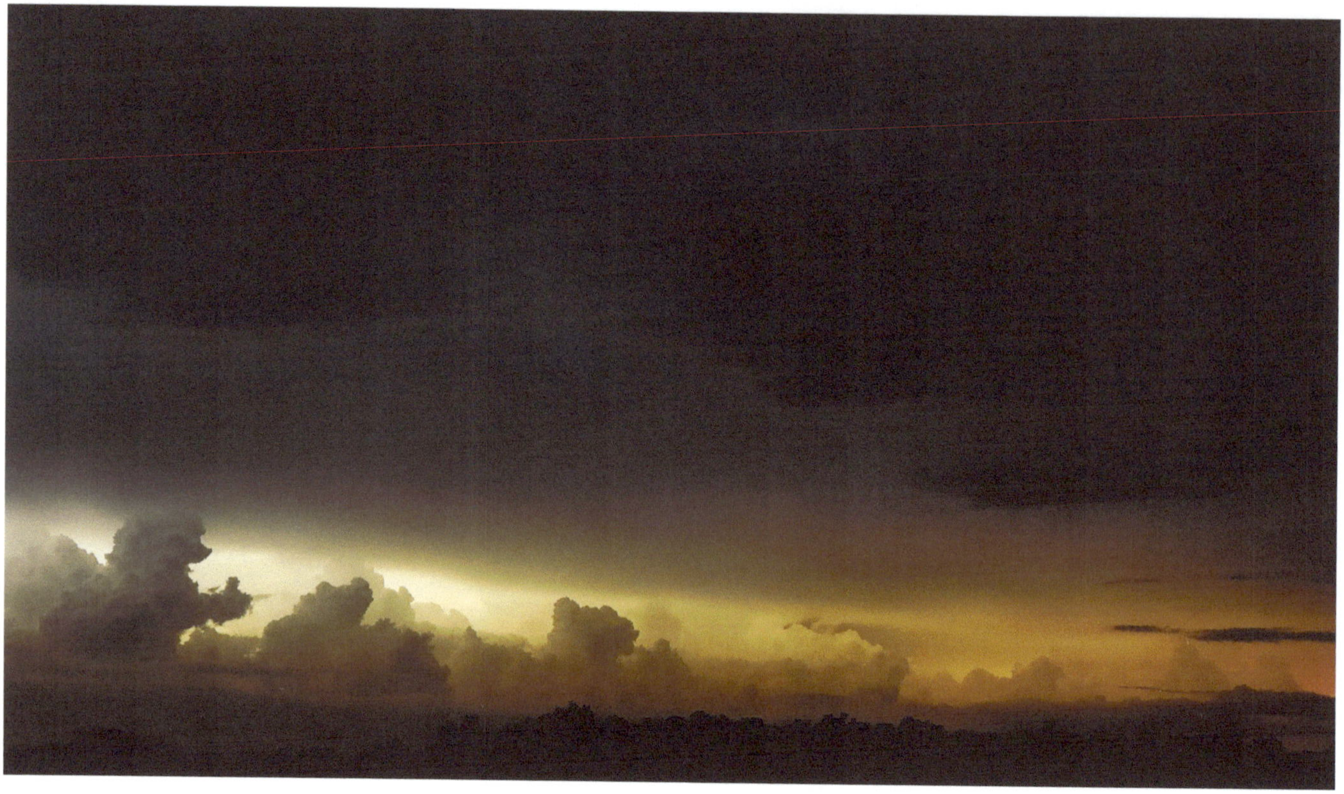

the most unsettling of seasons
raven storms threaten
the white skies of our order

I start to wake more often
to slate skies and a dimmed sun
the stage is set, the band is tuned
for the tempests yet to come

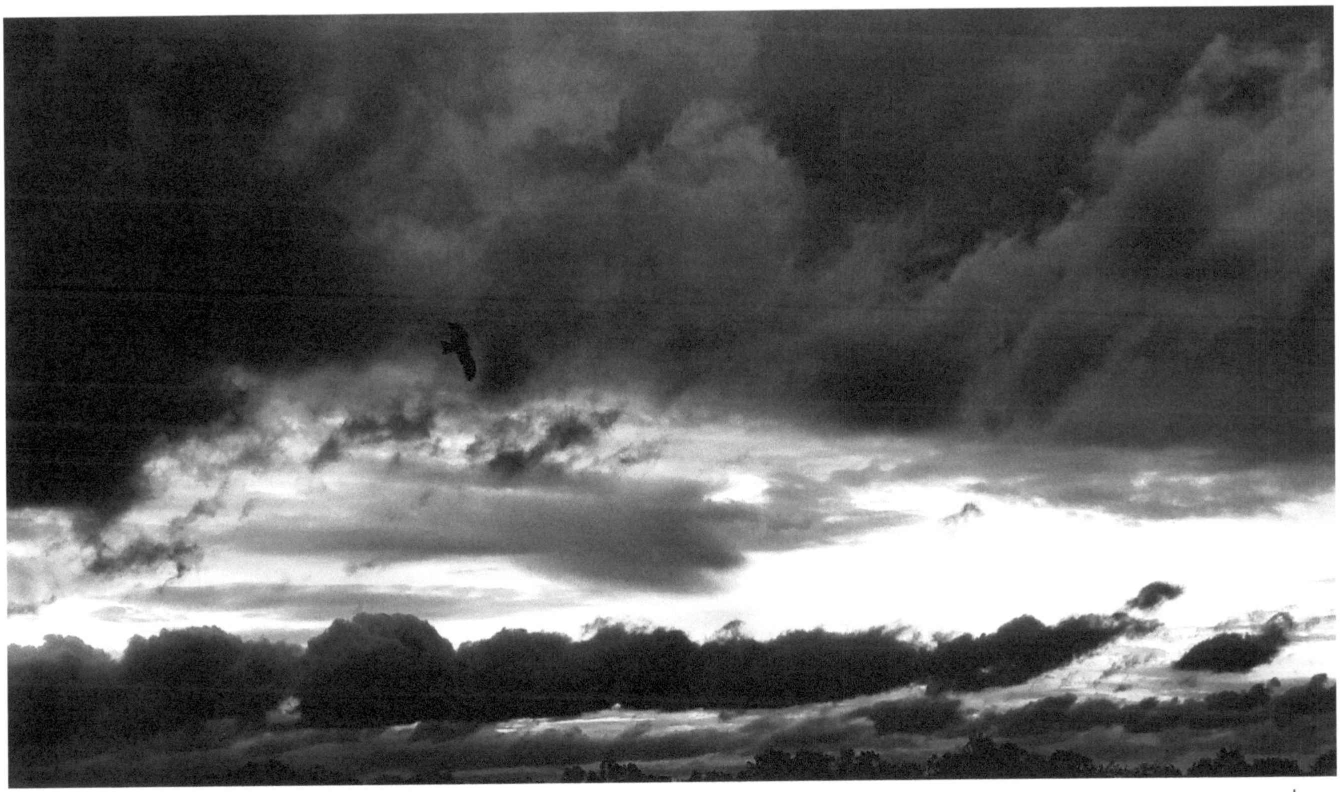

I hadn't seen one play out in years
tall shiny office buildings
are built to shut you in
and shut everything else out

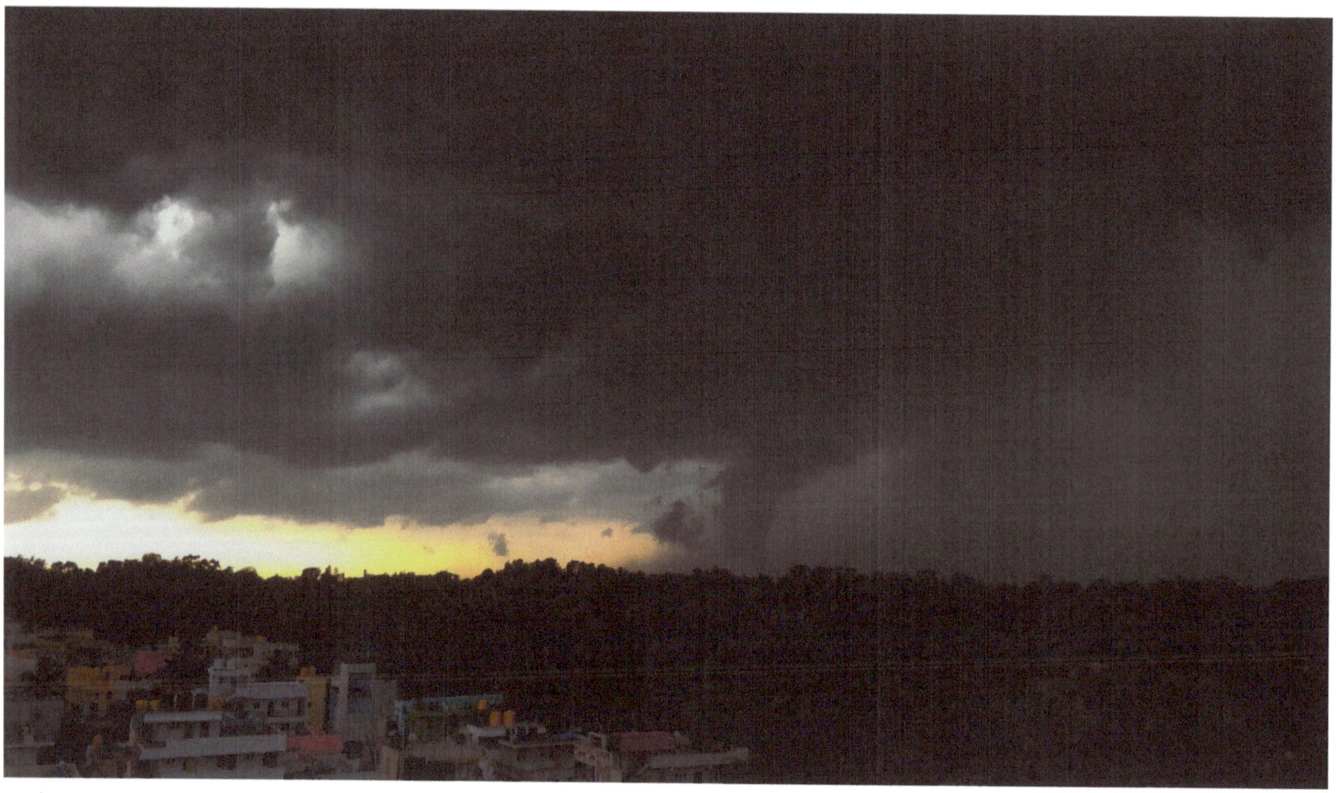

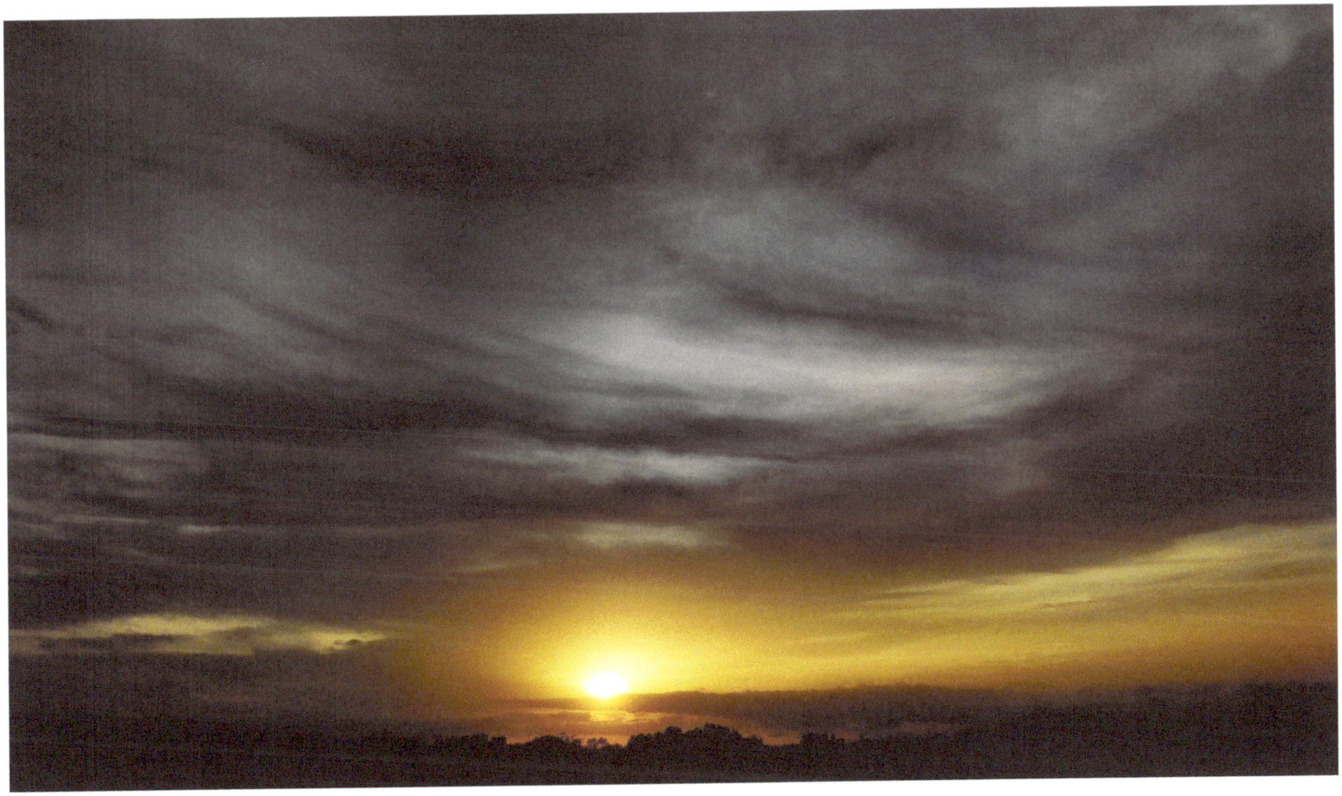

stepping out at day's end
finding rain on the ground
the only evidence of a storm
that has come and gone—
with I none the wiser

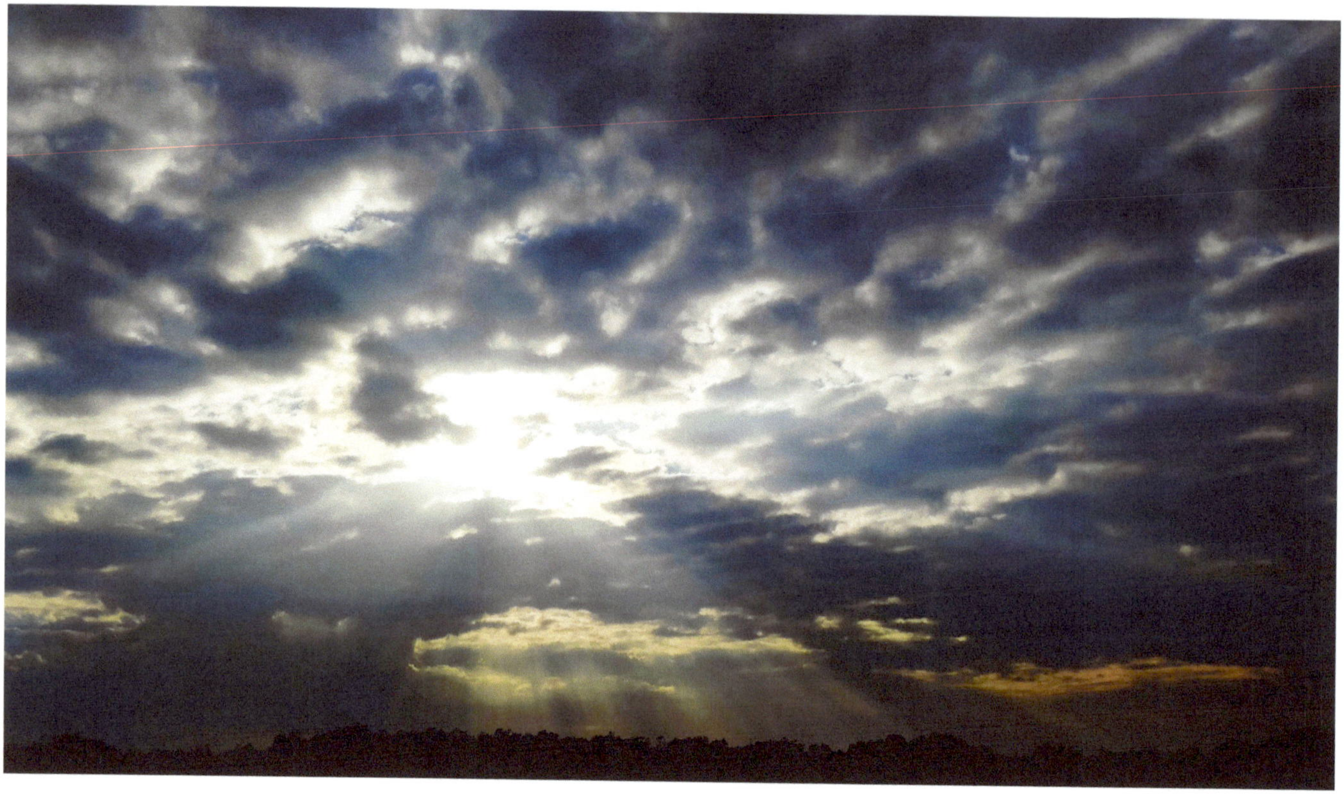

fascinating to watch
an approaching storm
as it swallows up
the vast, gleaming sky

the treetops swayed
as if choreographed
to the direction
of the gale force winds

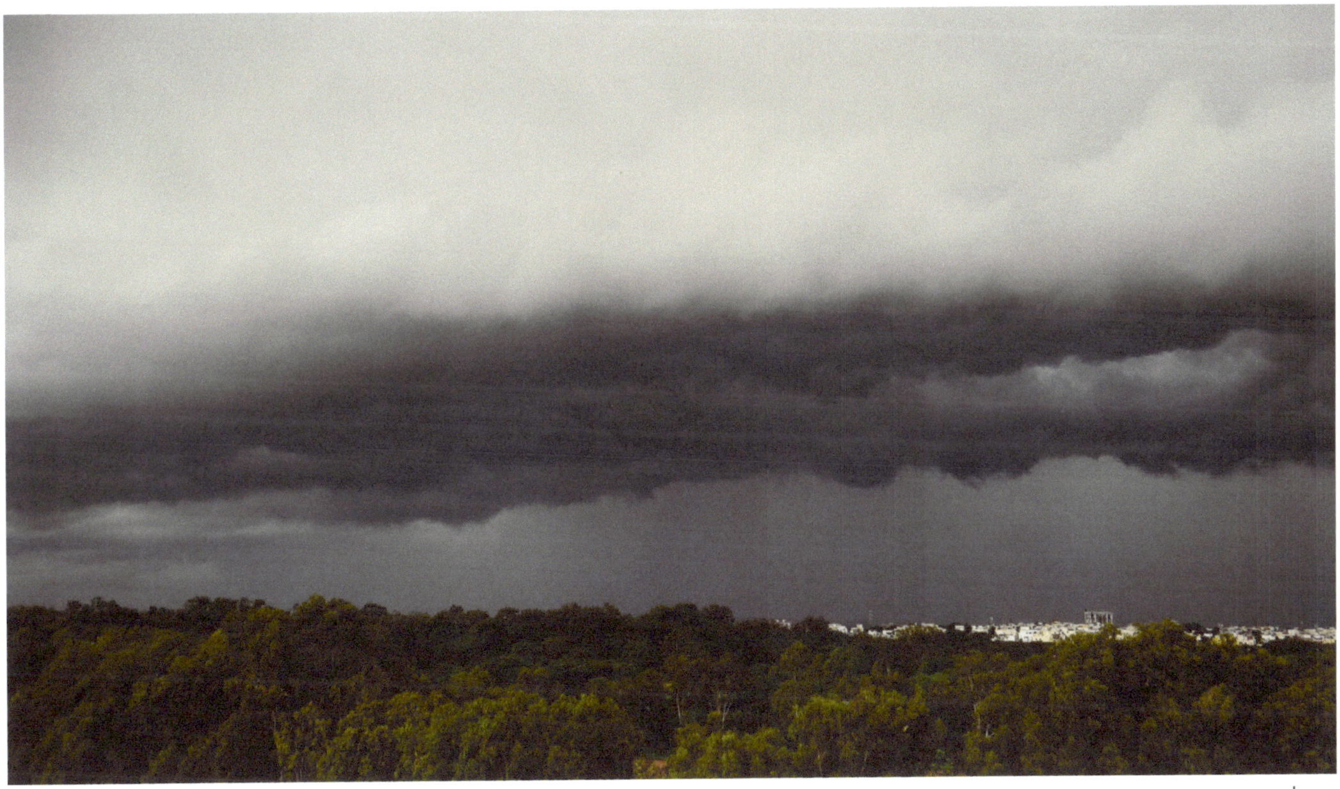

heralding the arrival
of grim, angry clouds
that blew in helter-skelter
from all directions

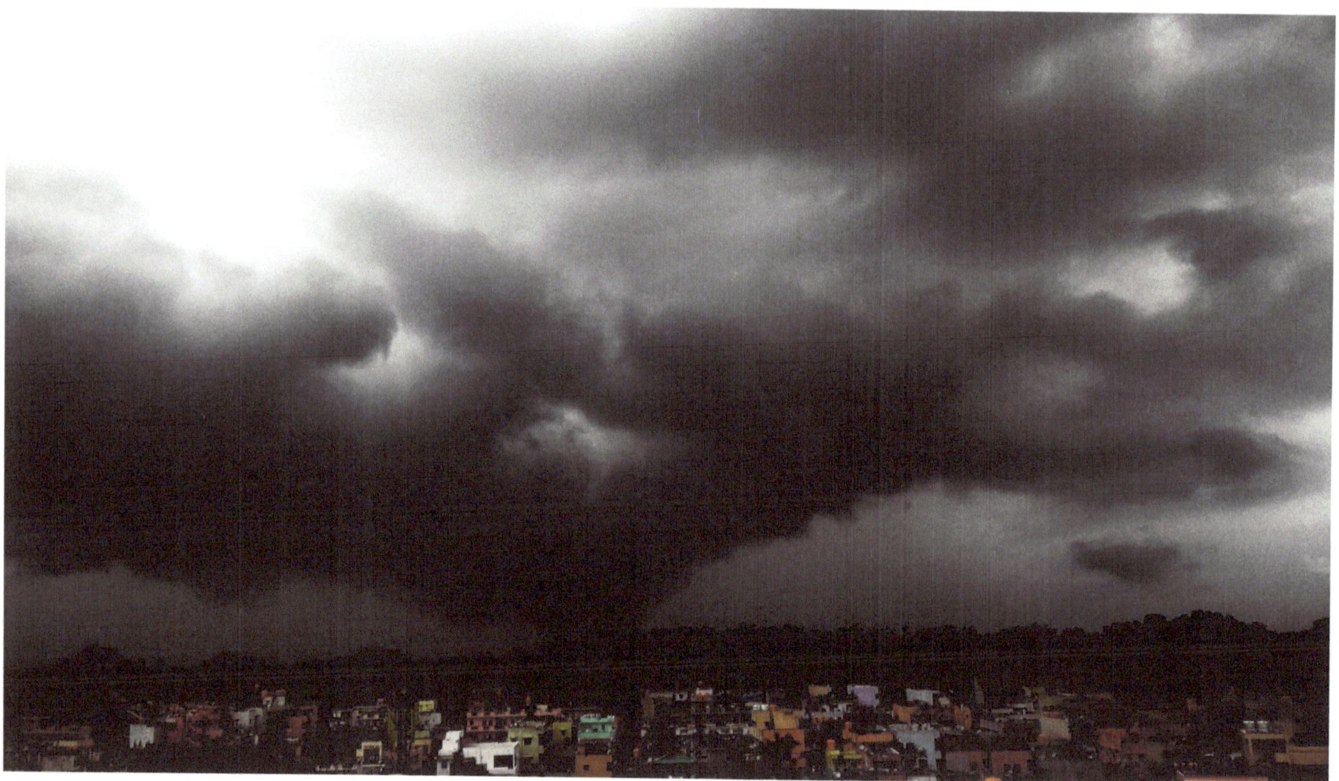

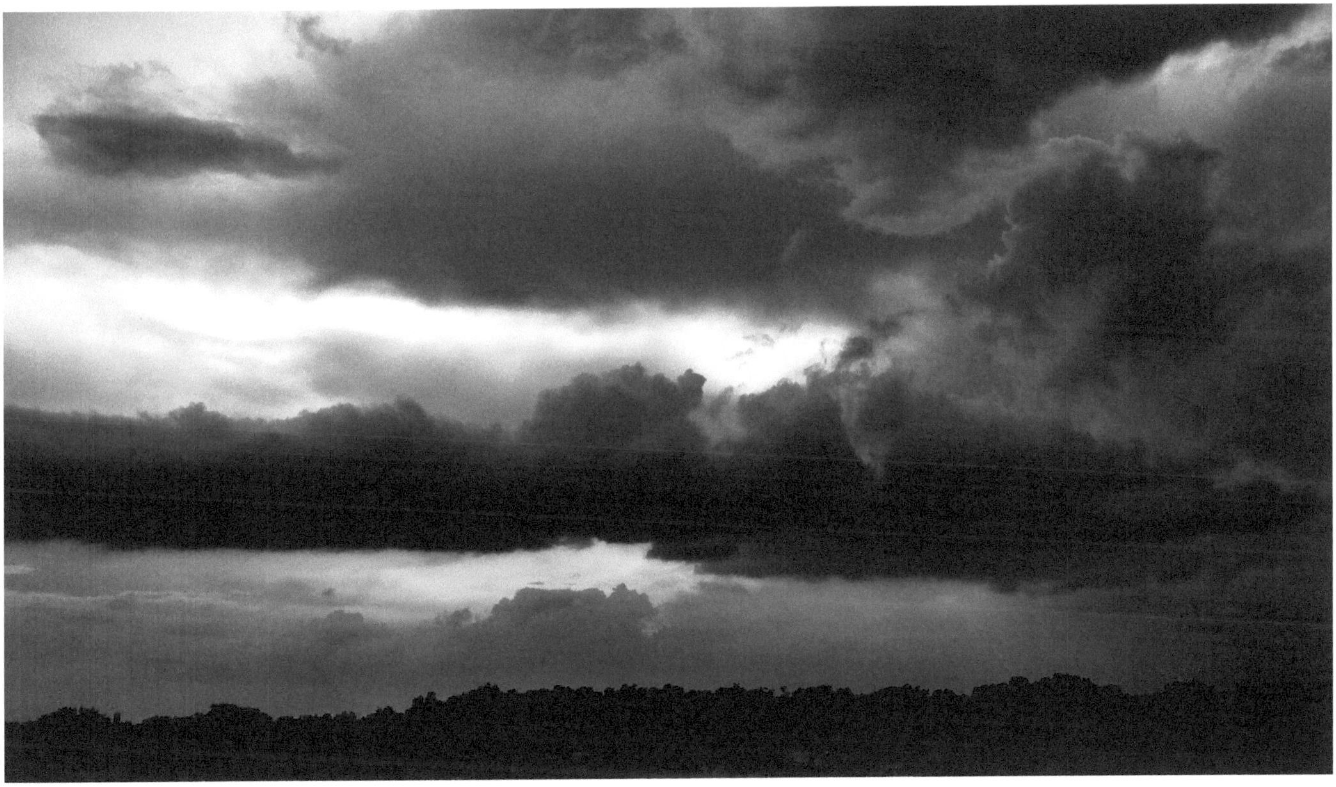

intent on closing up
even the smallest gap
through which the sky
could peep through

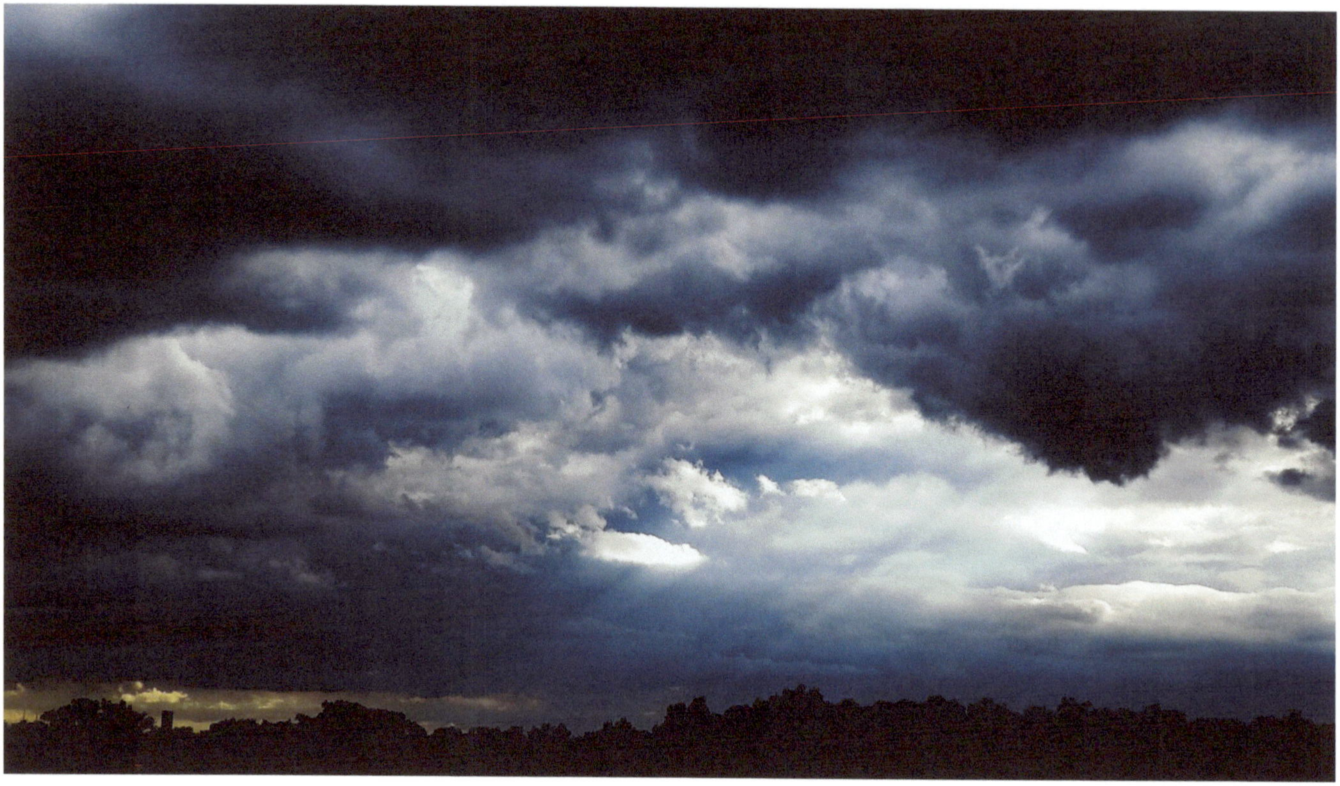

I watched them engulf
the cheery white and blue
with a threatening cloak
of unrelenting grey

on which lightning drew
myriad fantastical patterns
as thunder roared
like a background score

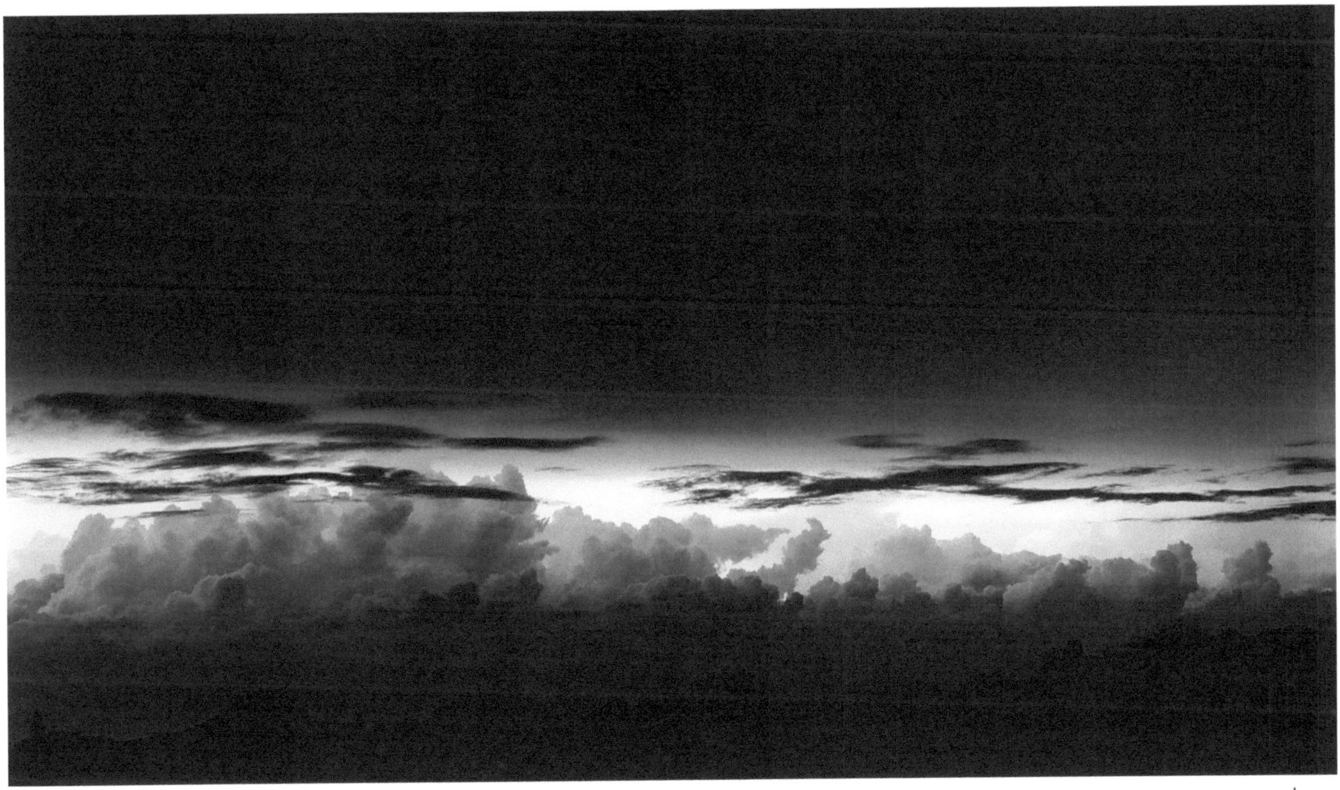

and how the rain poured
as if sprung from a source so deep
its end could never be reached—
but end it did

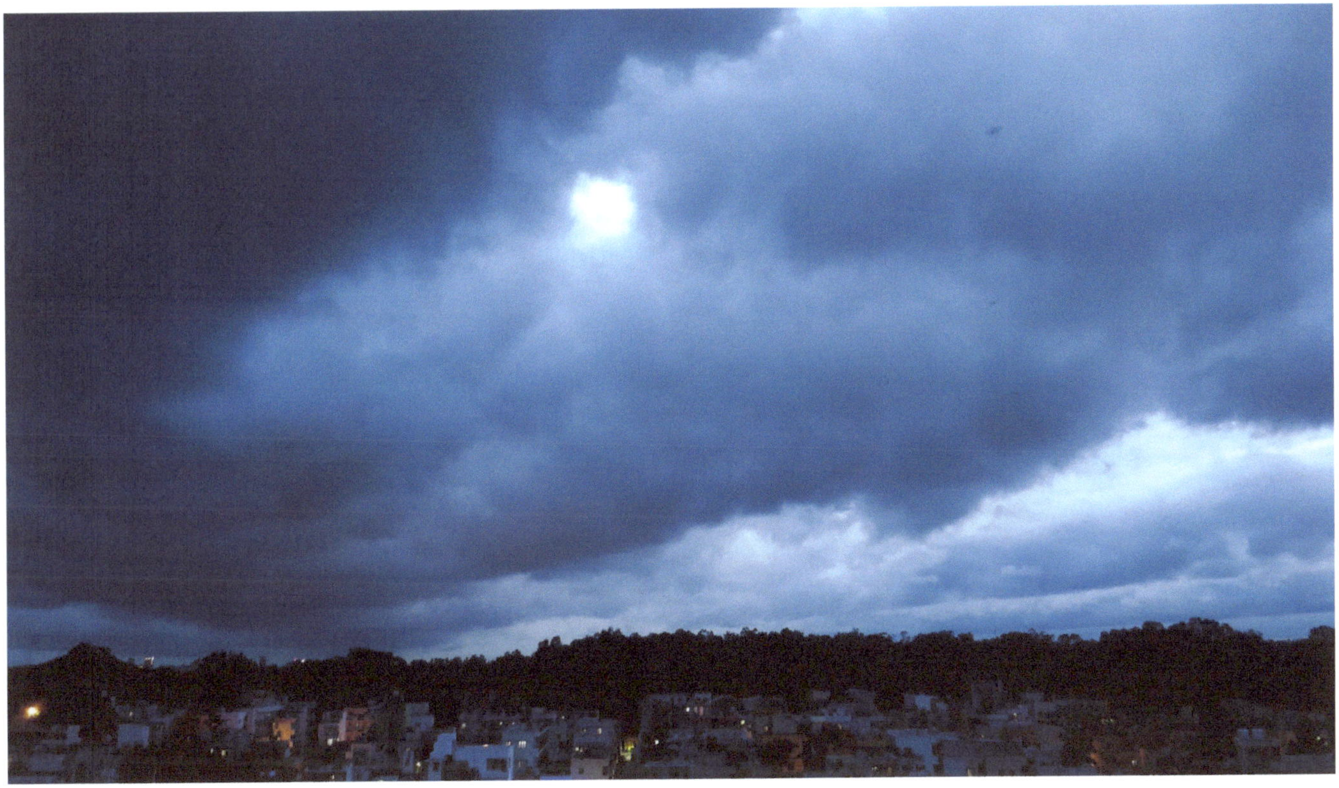

while those clouds
that felt so omnipotent
as they rendered
their elemental dance

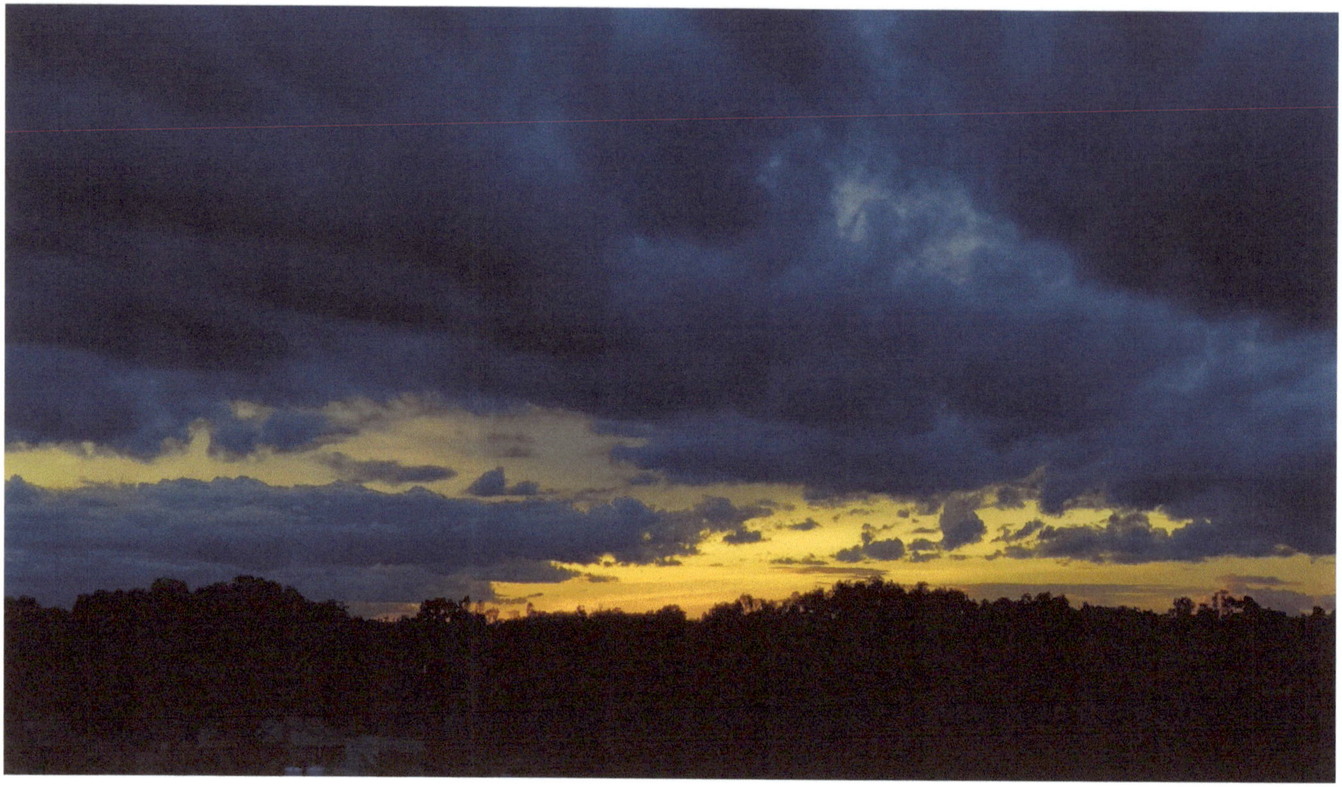

had to make way
at last
for the blue and white
once again

I made a promise then
to remember that,
the next time I woke up
to a day that felt endless...

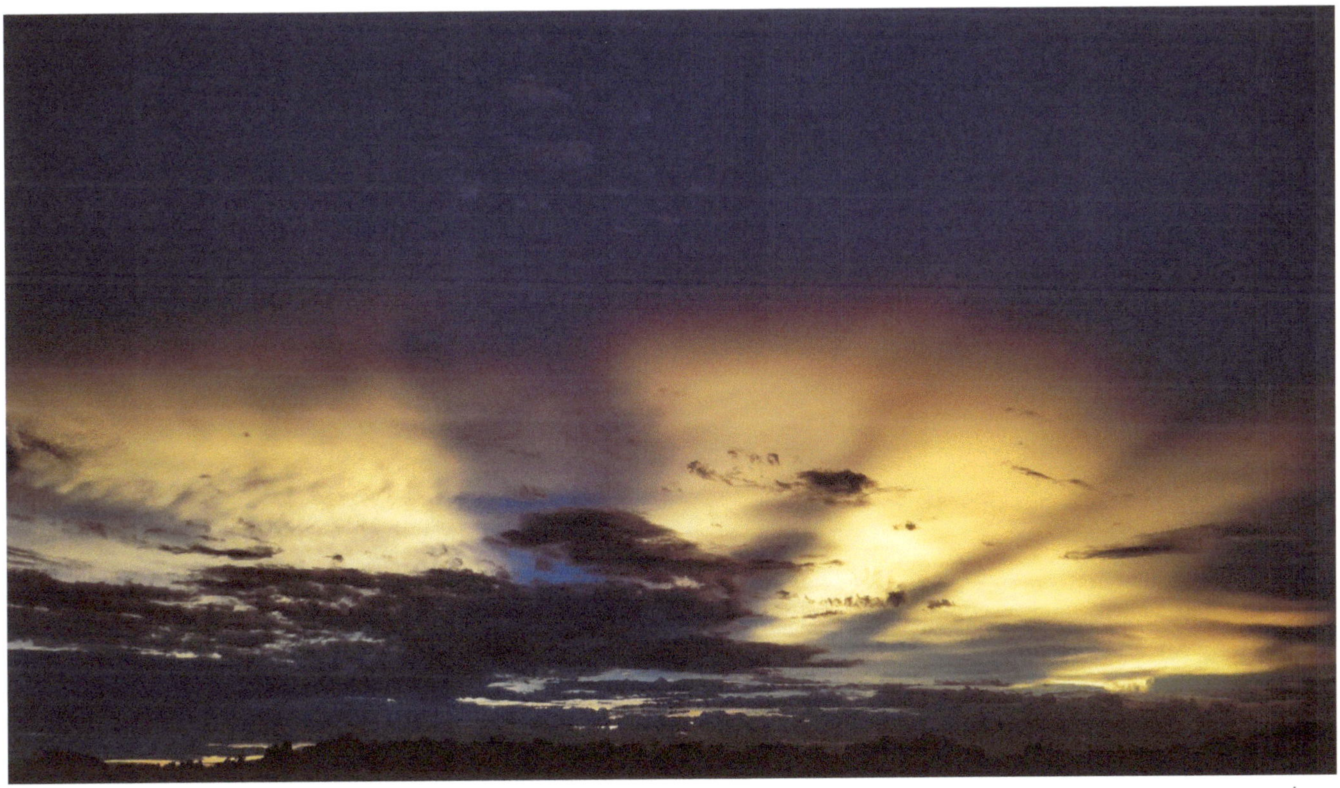

when days stack into forever
normal seems a distant shore
when looking ahead is uncertain
you finally look around for more

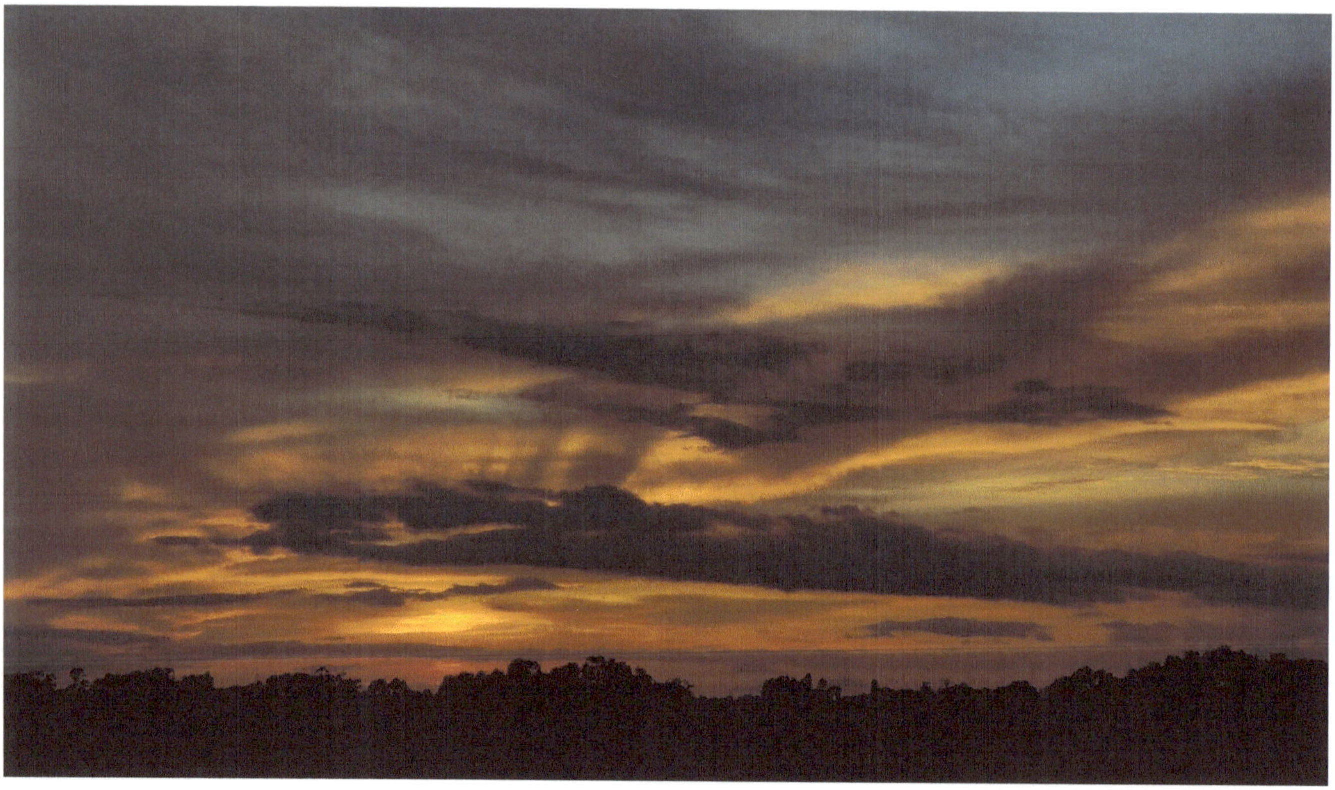

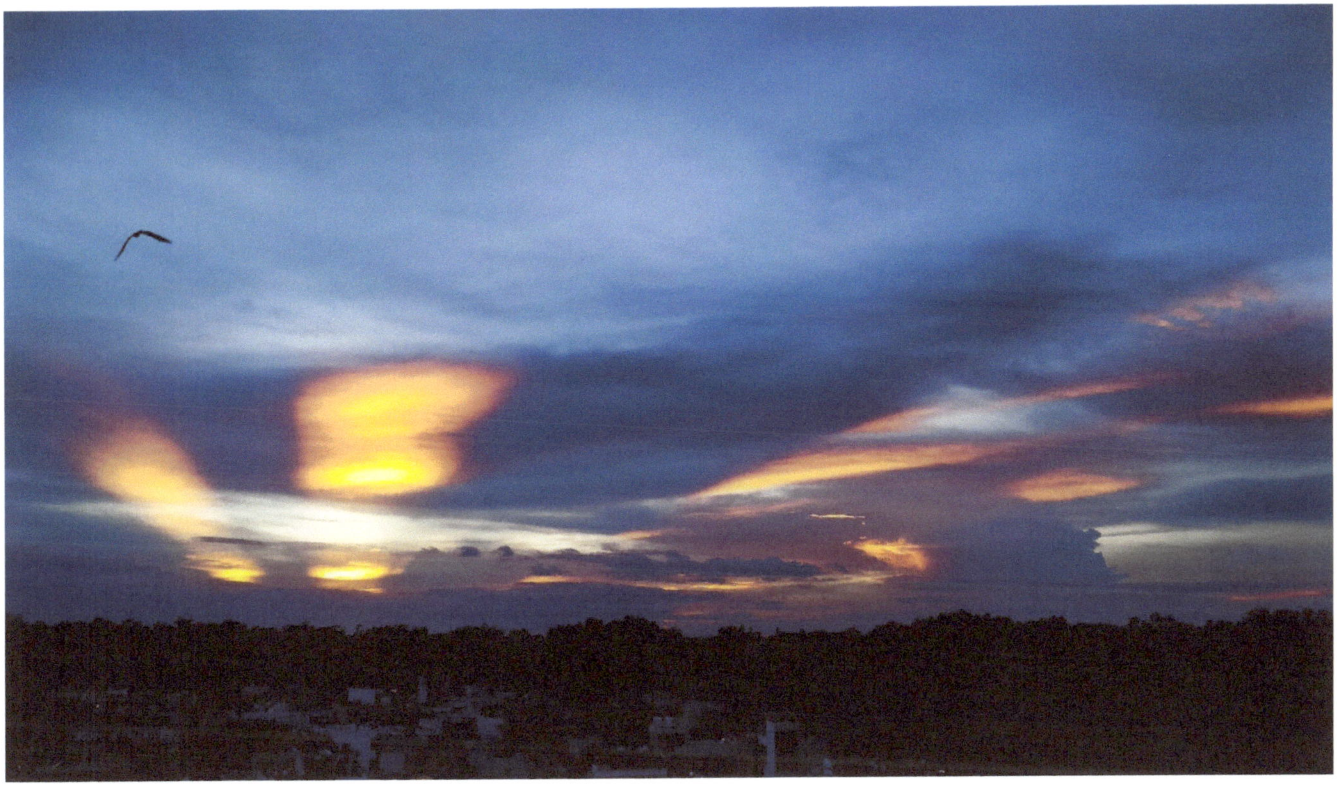

I looked toward the rooftops
as life unchained from time
where paper kites were launched
by hands both old and young

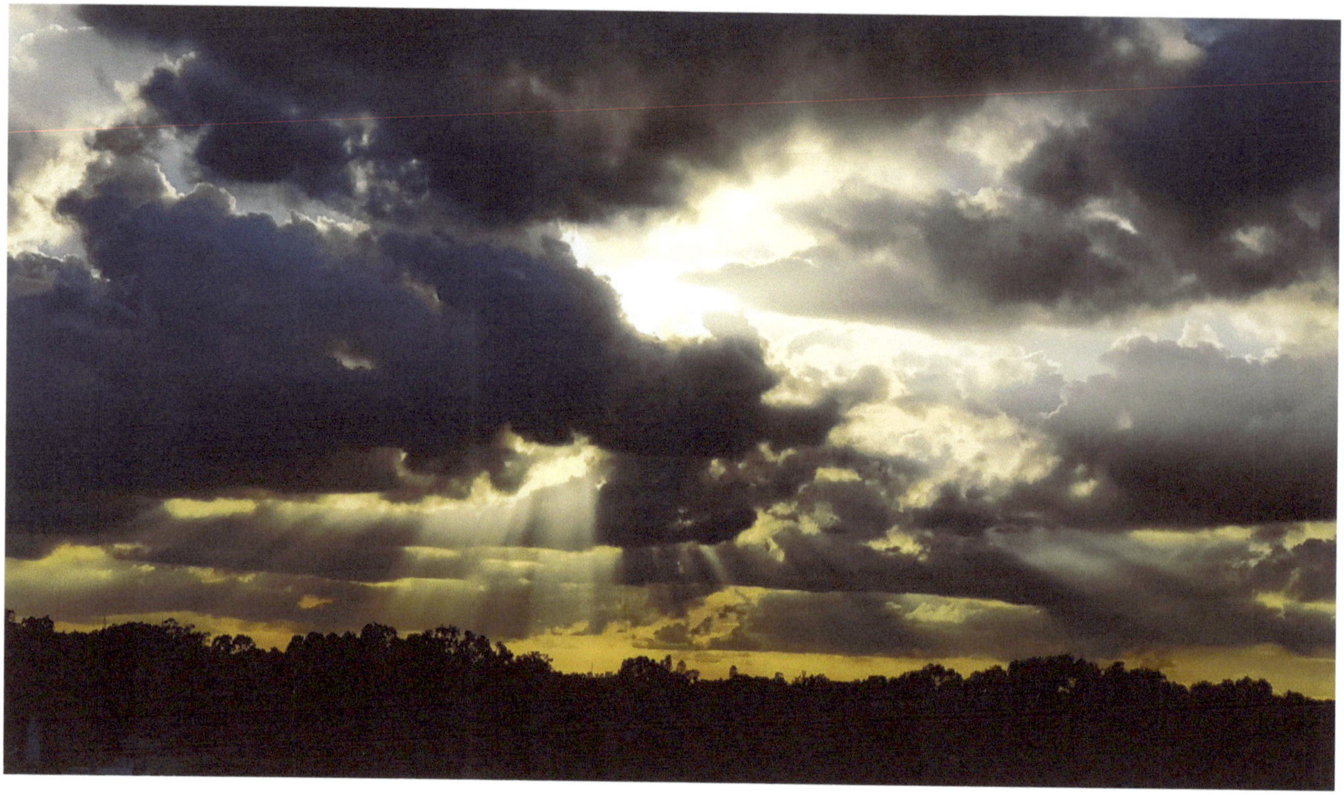

I looked at the roads
where raindrops pooled
and recalled the joy
of gumboots splashing puddles

I looked up and wondered when
I stopped gazing at clouds
to find the shapes they hide
a castle here, a dragon there

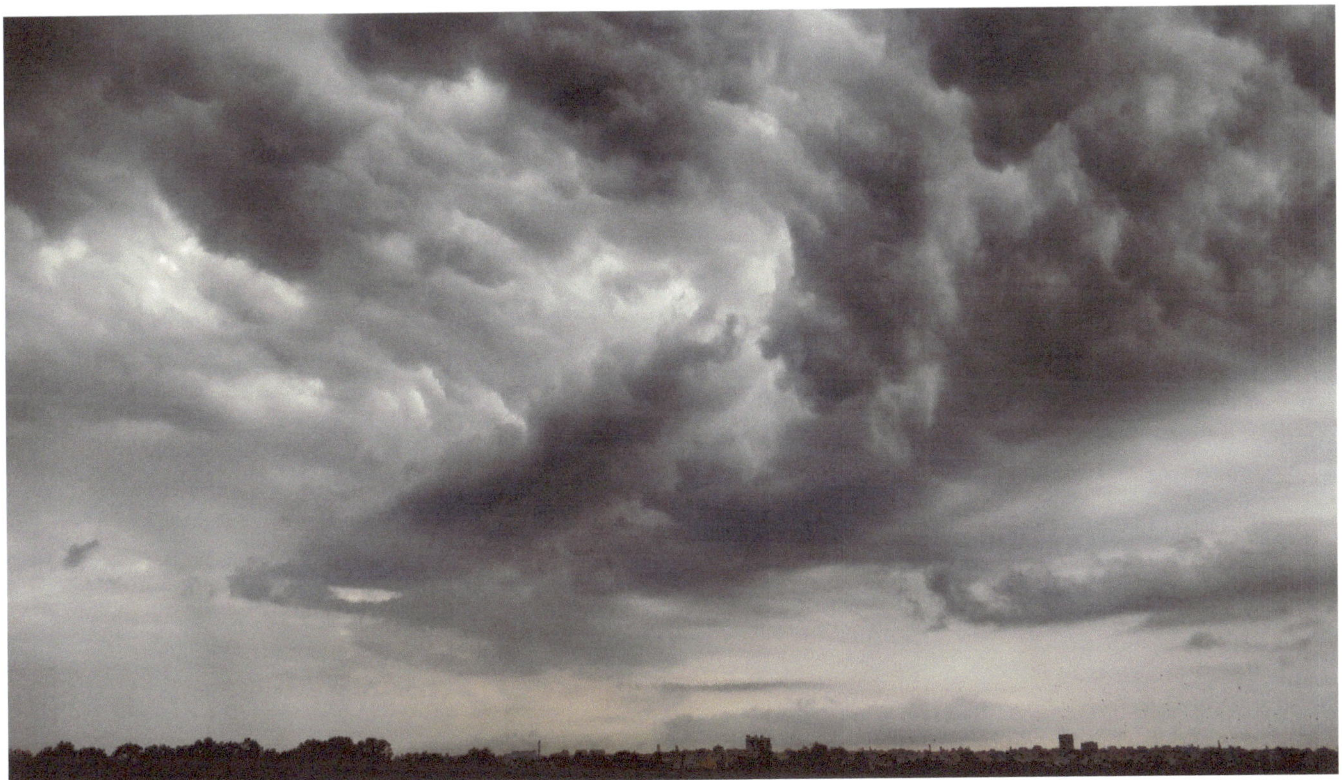

had bees always stopped by
a hair's breadth from my window
with that enquiring attitude
as if scoping real estate

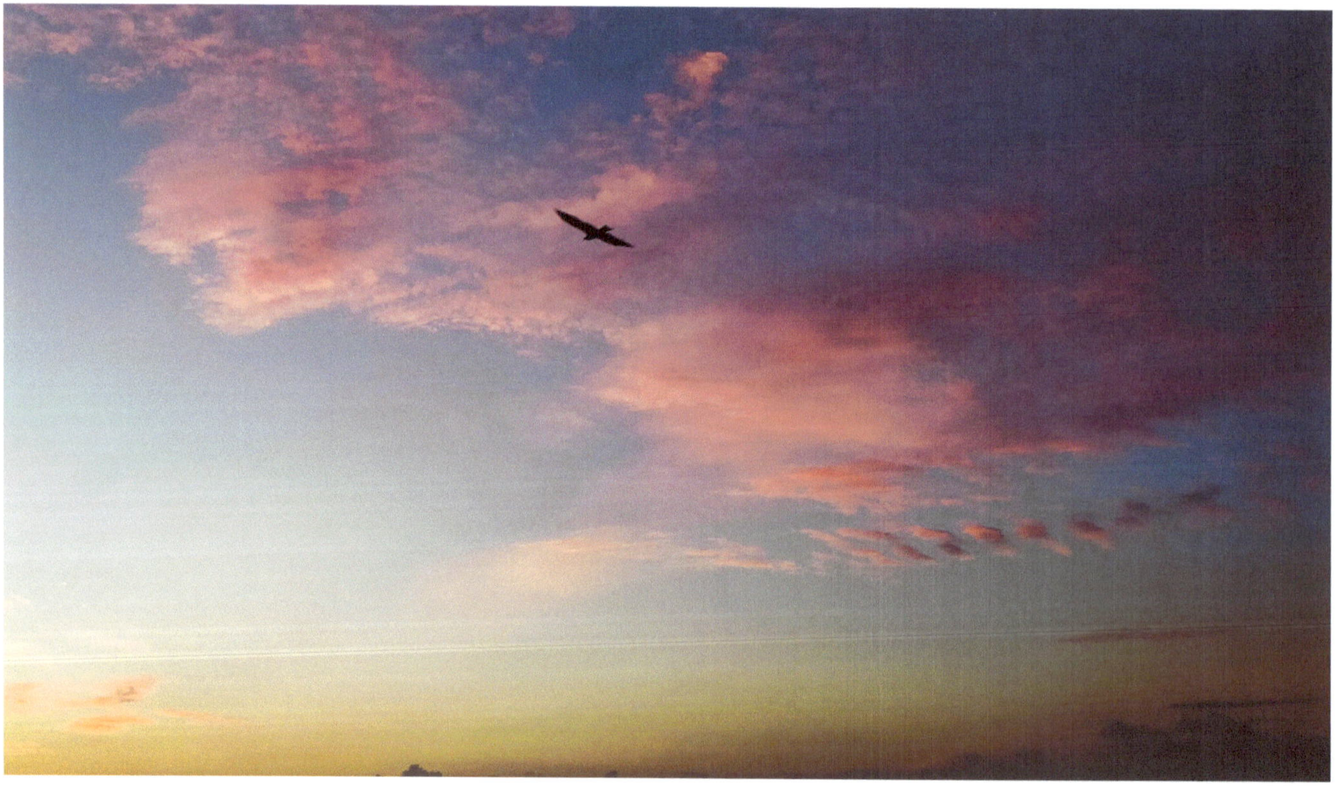

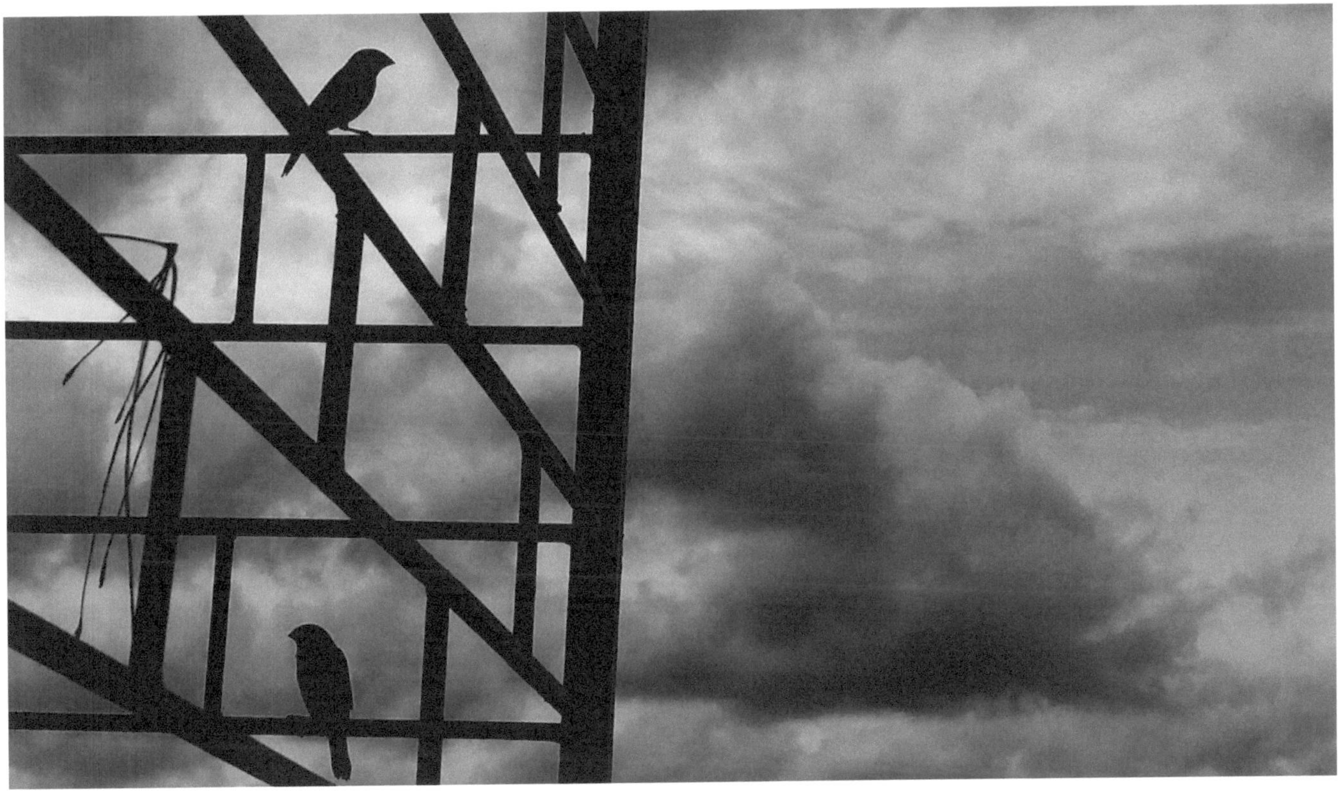

had birds always settled
their domestic disputes
on my balcony railing
in my line of vision

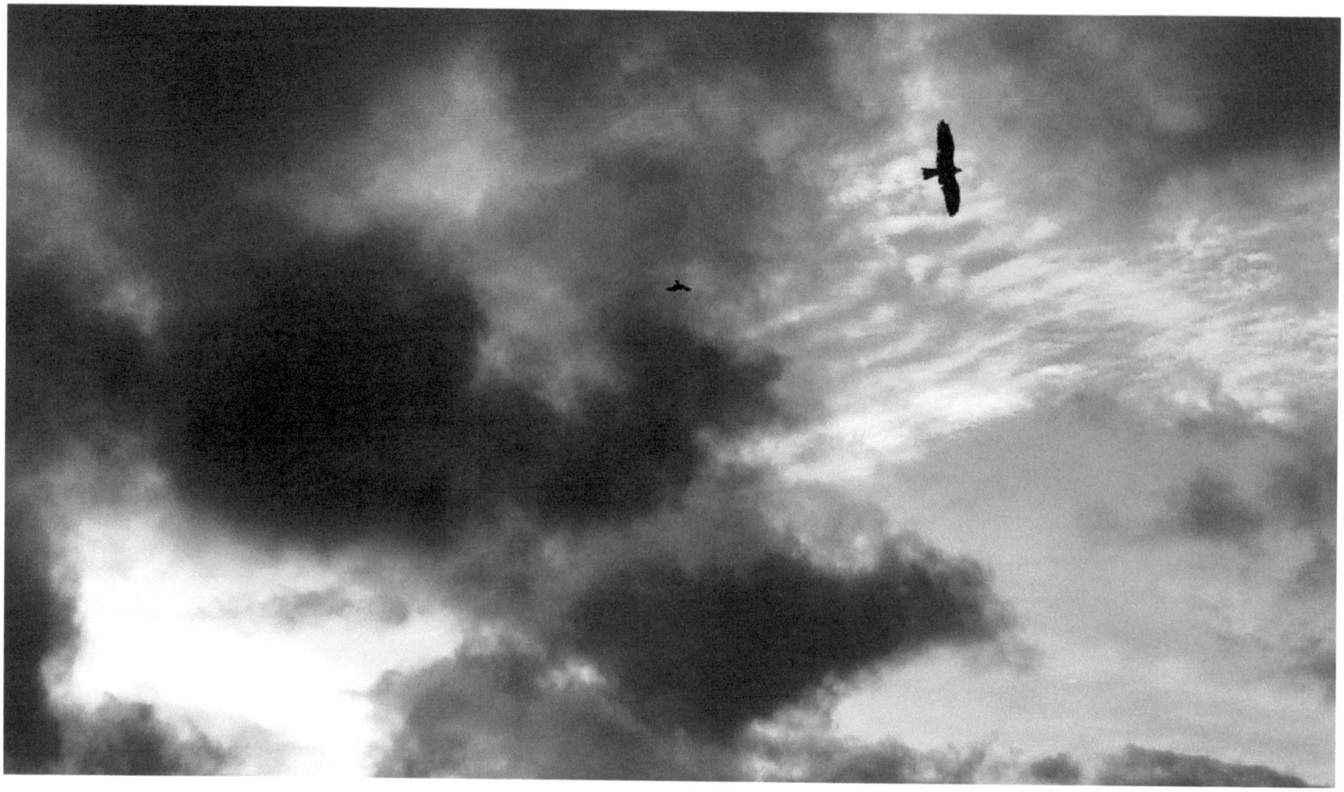

had eagles always used
my roof as a diving platform
I suppose they had
my curtains were always drawn

but by far the biggest delight
was when I stumbled upon
sunsets…
hidden in plain sight

who knew sunlight could fracture
in a million beautiful ways
when forced to find its way through dark clouds
that seek to bury its colour
in watery grey

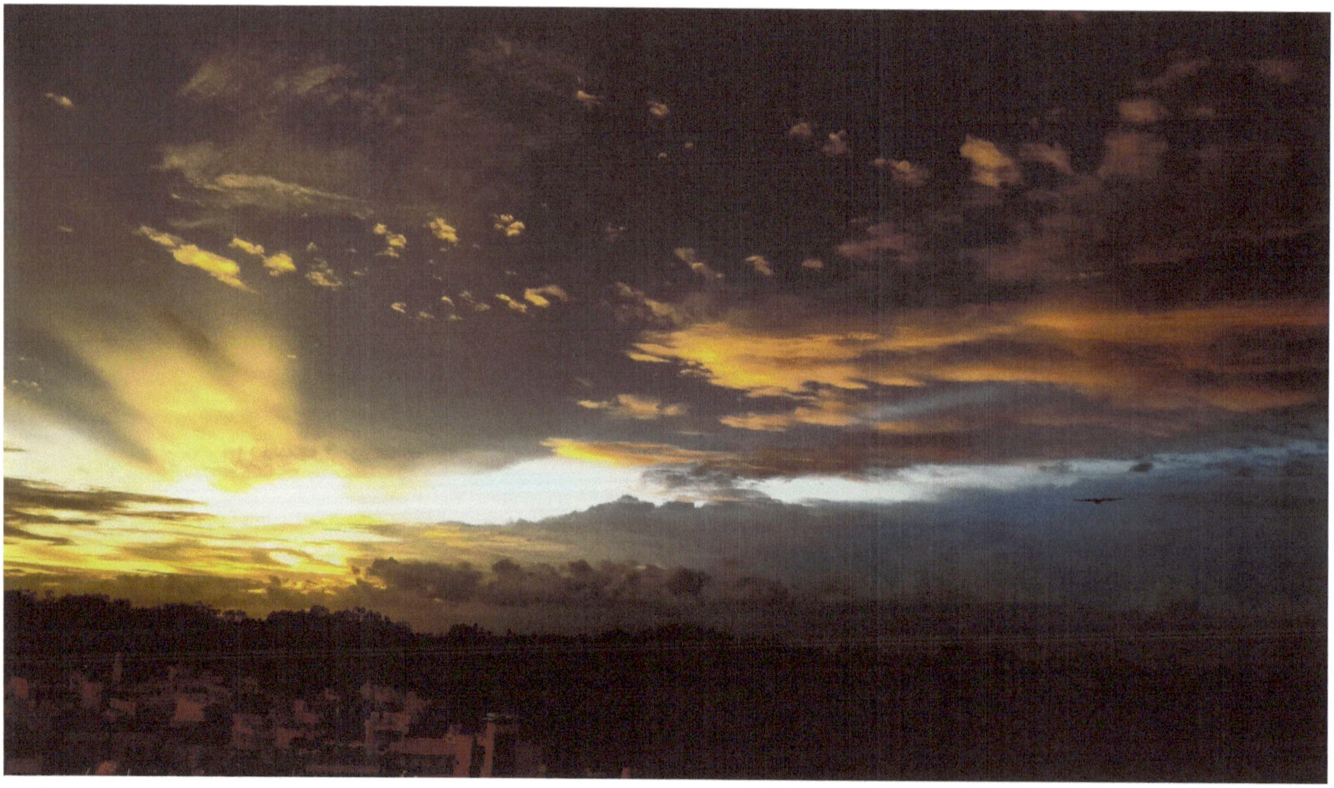

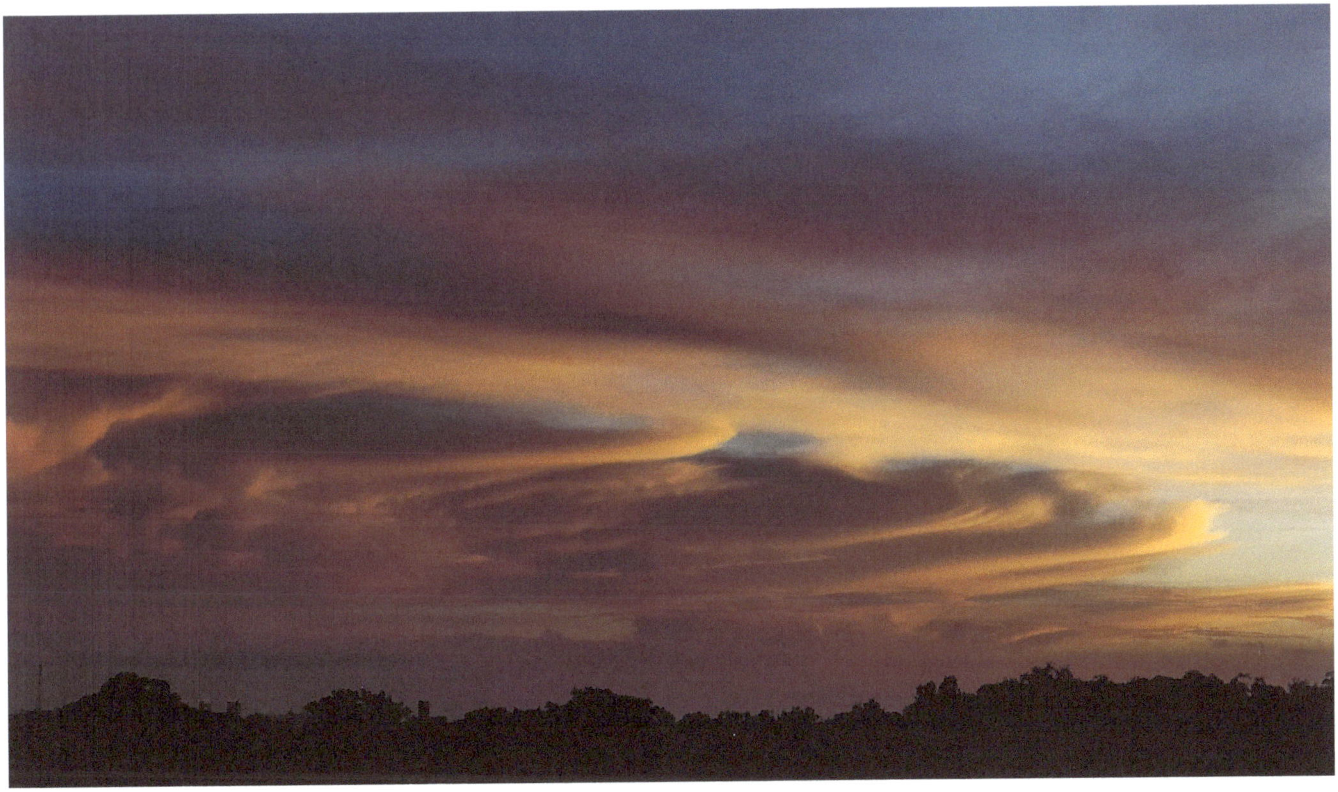

onto my balcony
ten monsoons knocked and left
yet I never stepped out and looked to the west
in that narrow window
when the sun bids farewell

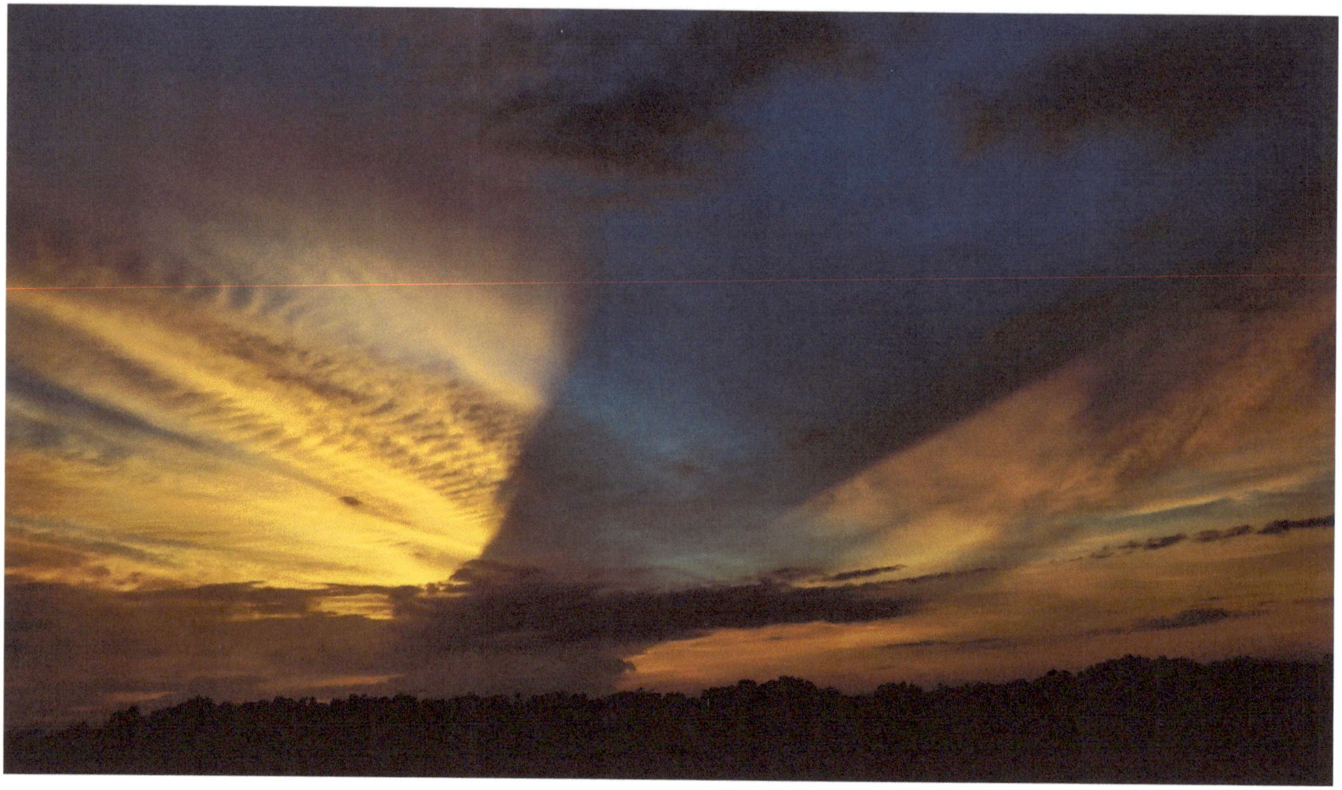

I never had the time
my day's pattern was set
in rigid lines, too ingrained
to accommodate change

I suddenly realised
how over the years
I packed up sunrises and sunsets
into a box labelled
"only seek on vacations"

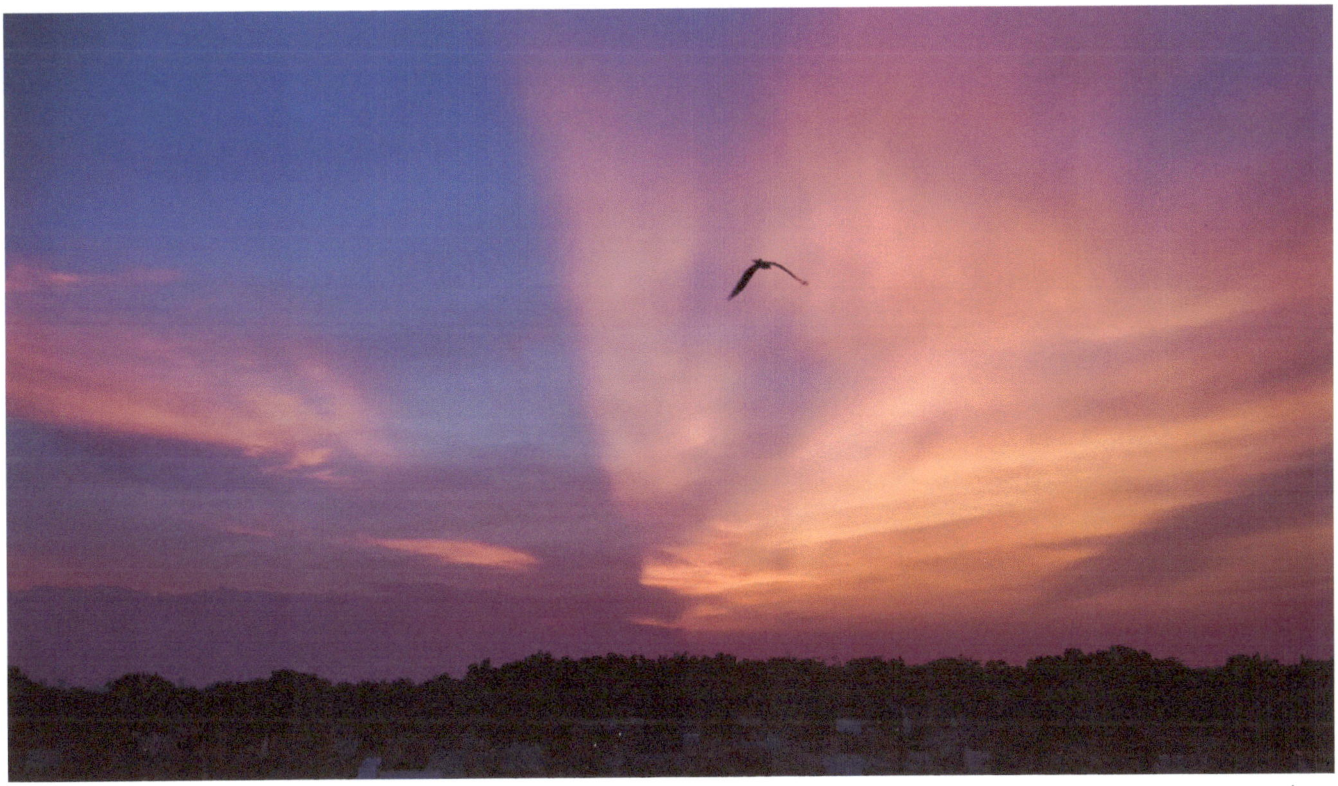

all the while unaware
my eyes were bereft
of what waited for me
if only I'd stepped out
and looked to the left

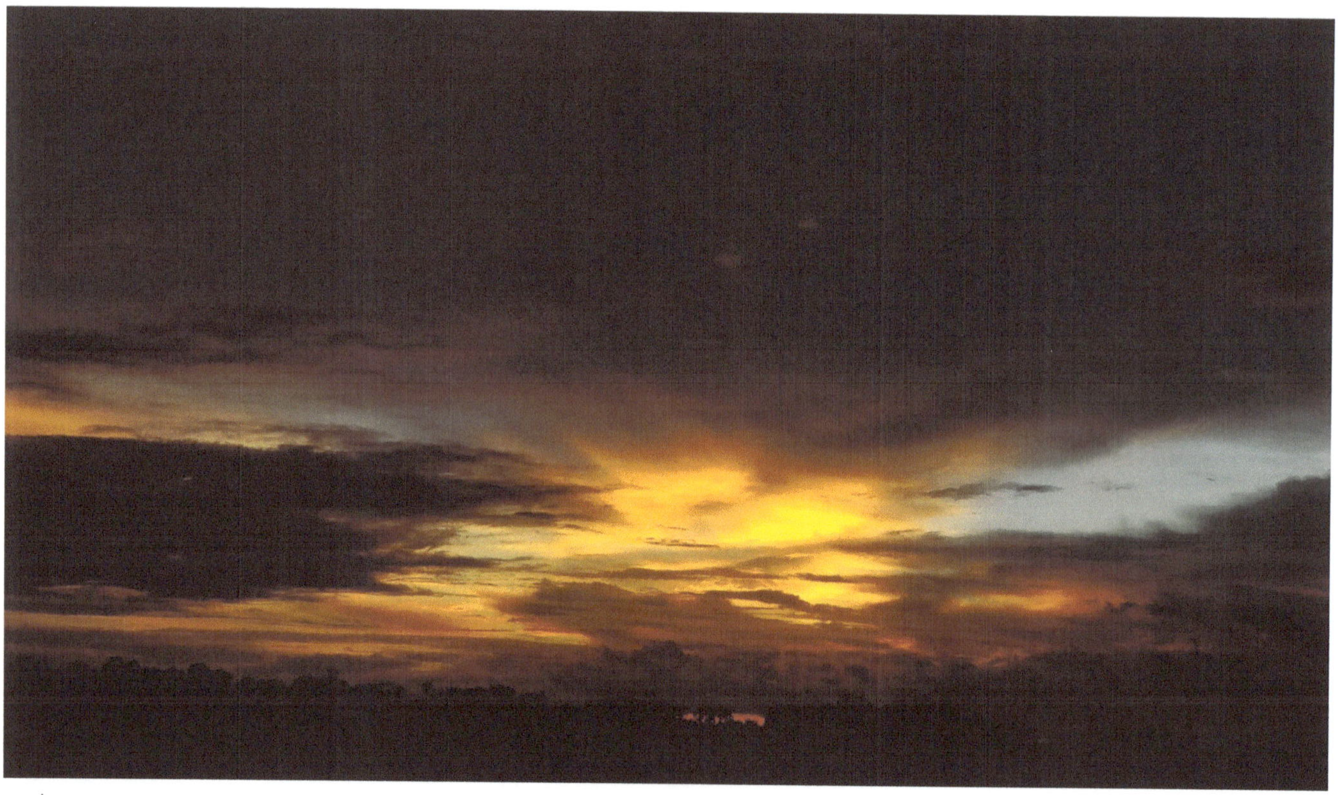

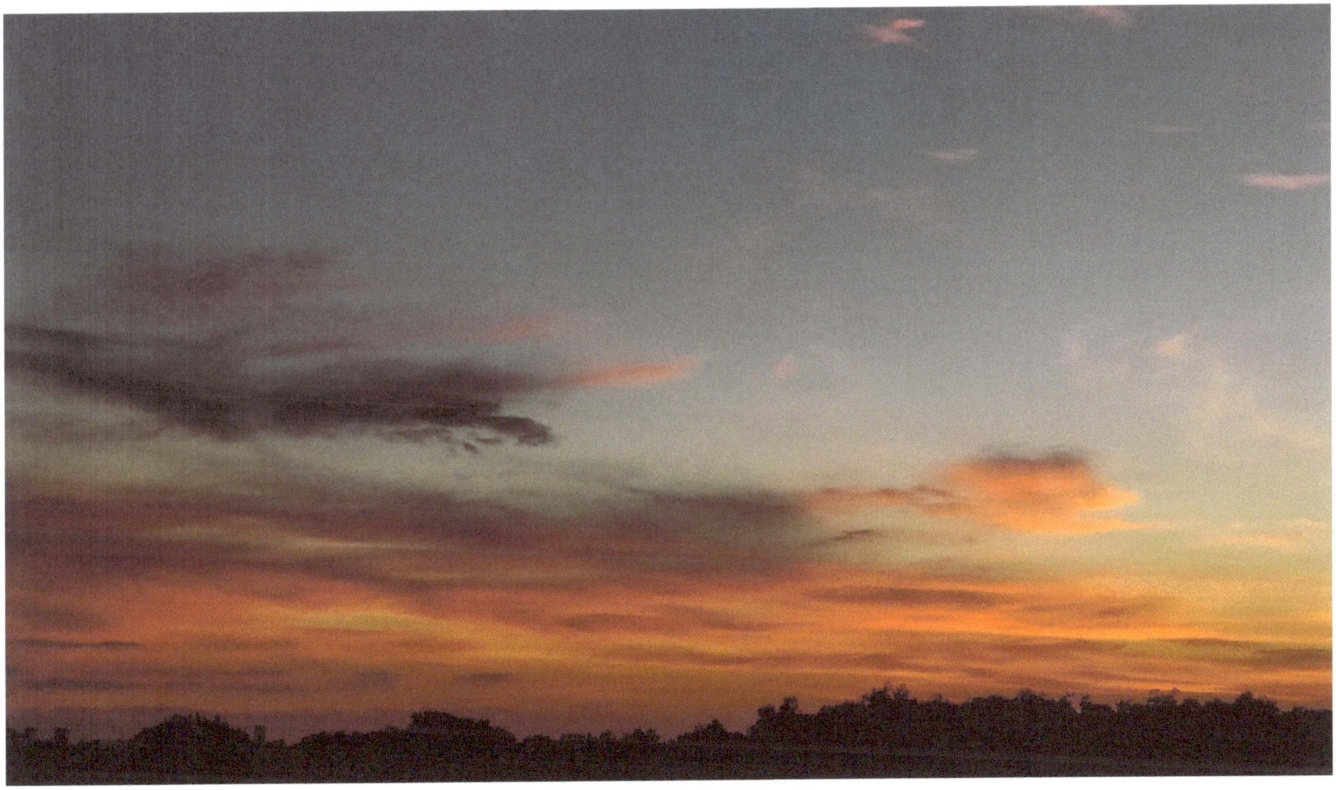

I watched it all now
and marvelled at the show
I watched it all now
with breaths, deep and slow

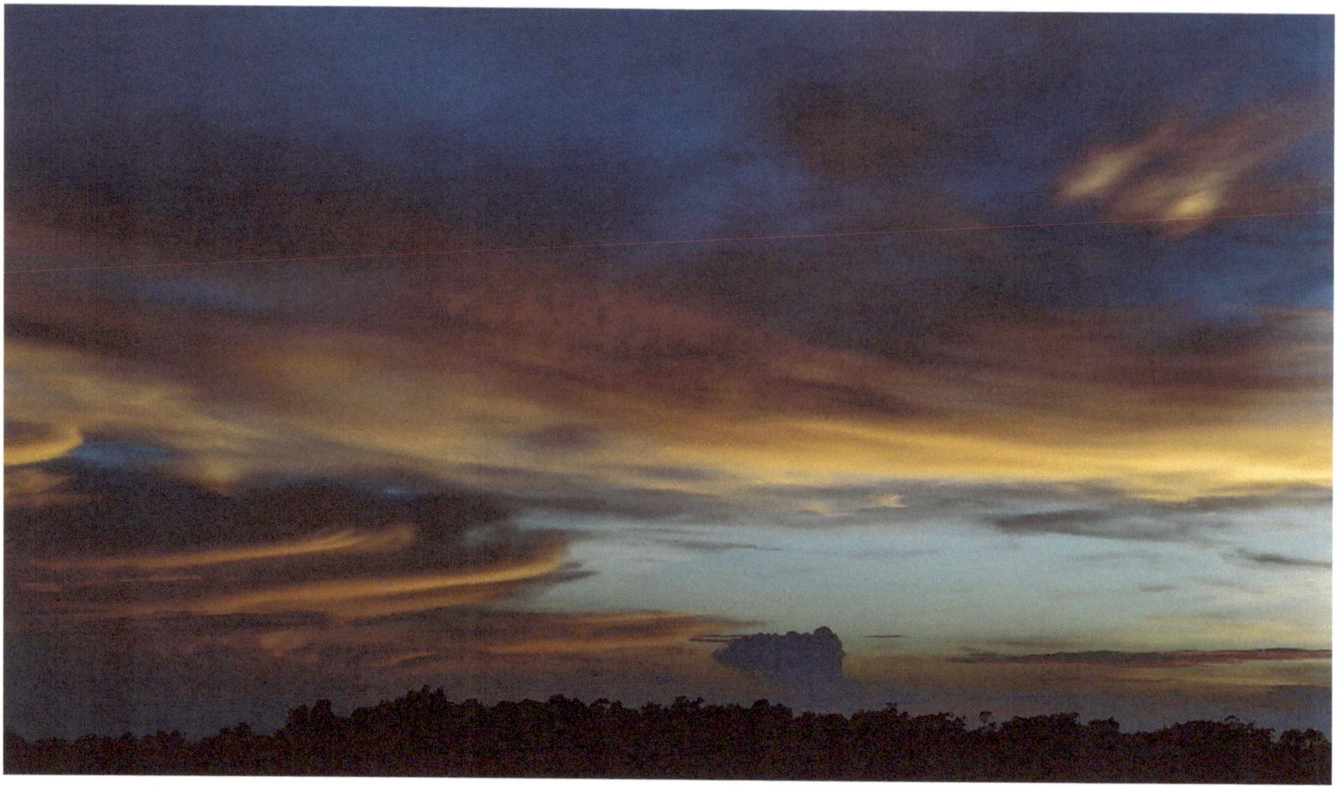

the world is put on pause
and before we press play
I hope we all catch on to
what we missed until today

as this tale draws to a close
the breeze no longer dances
to rain's fragrant tune
silent skies shiver at
approaching Winter's knell

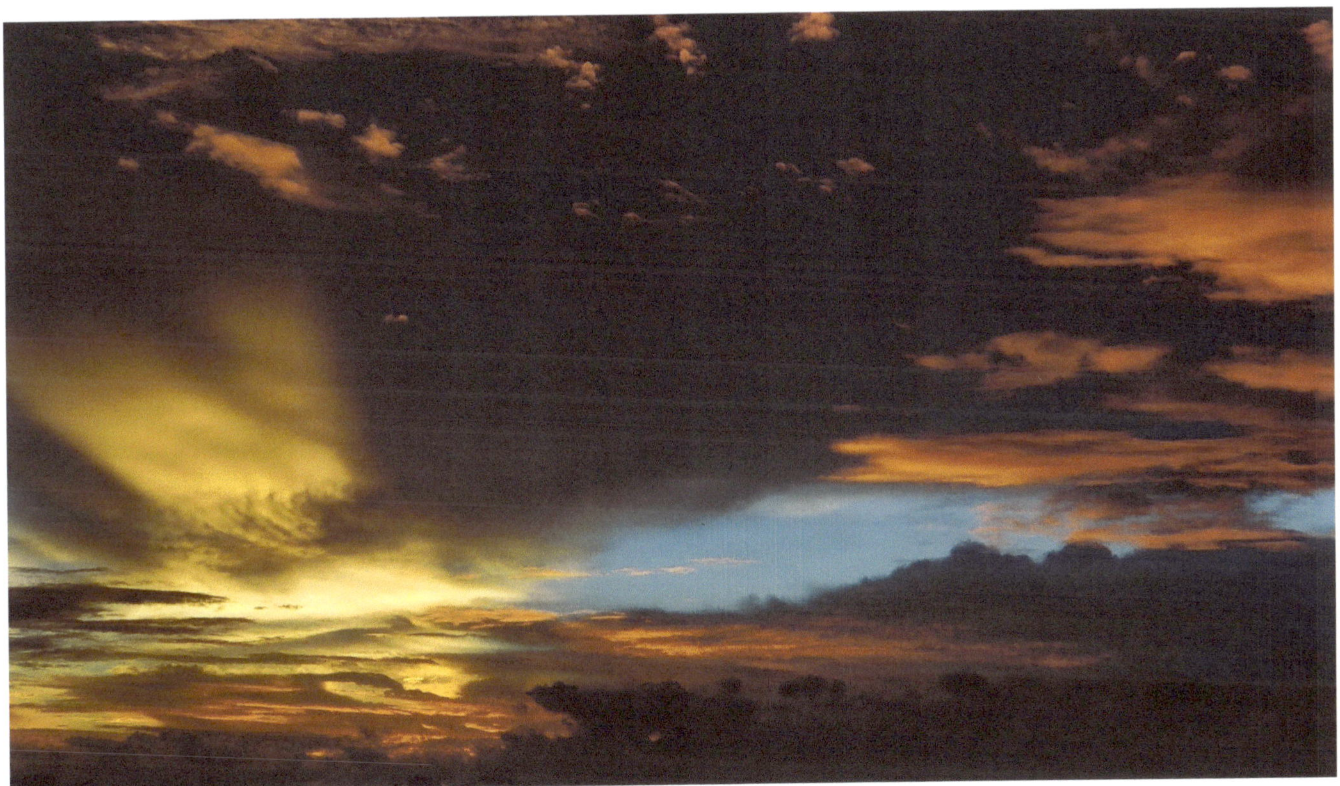

and were you to ask of me
words to remember it by
this is what they would be:

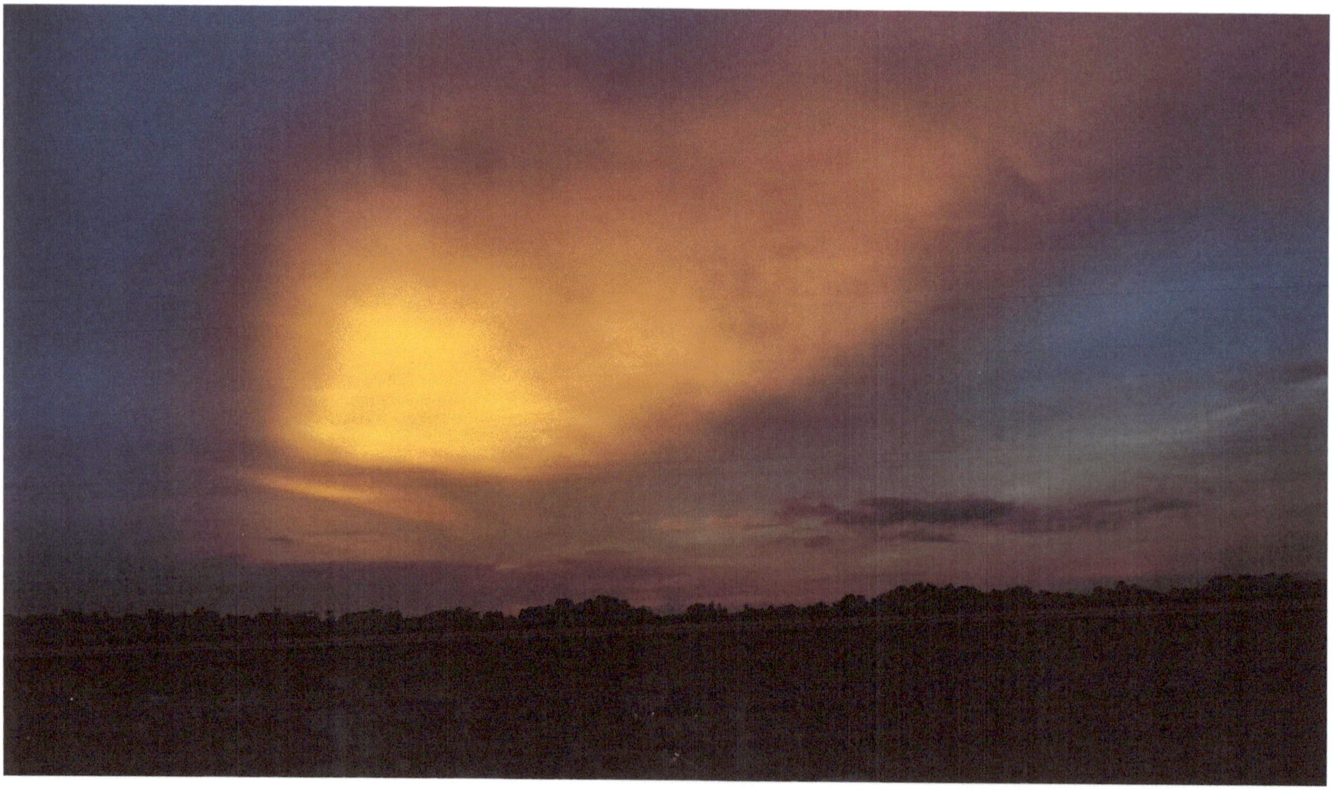

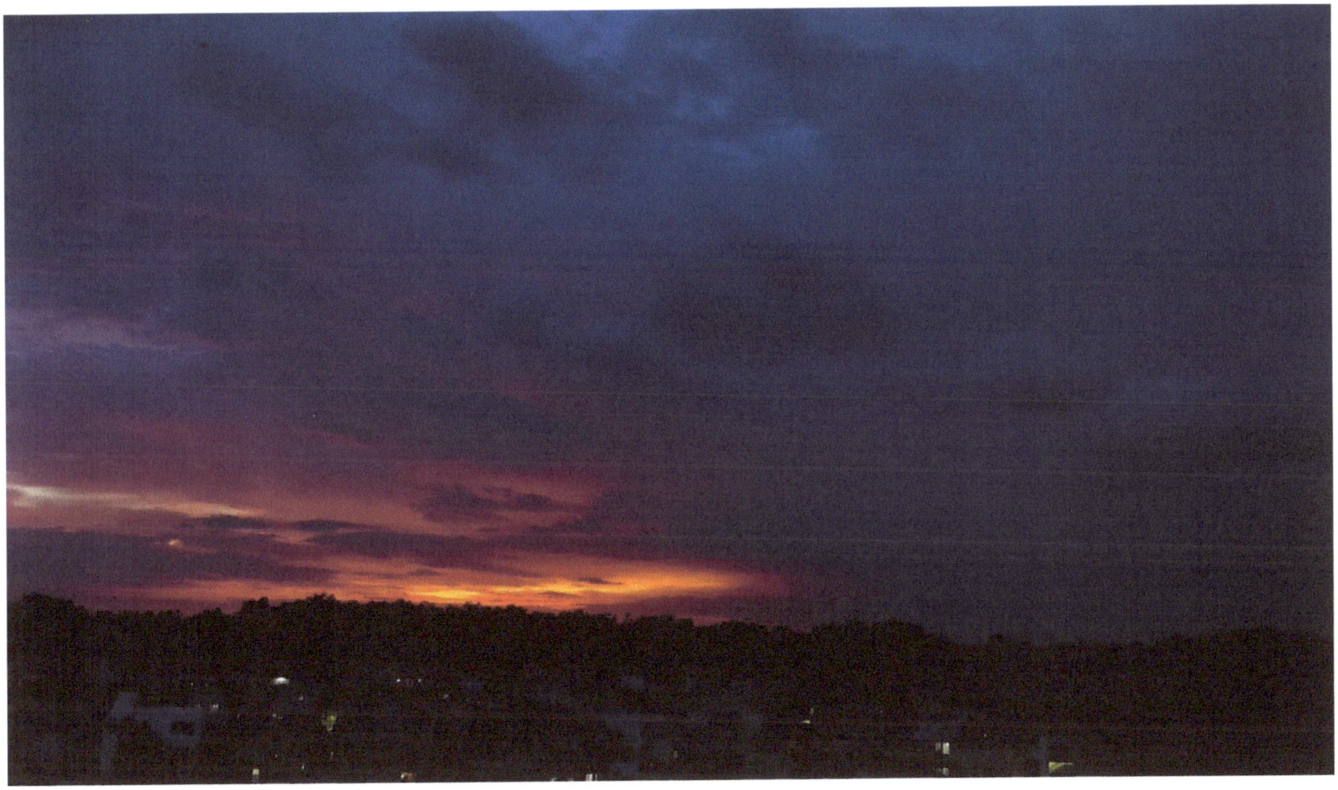

when nature paints
no colours ever clash
orange marries pink and blue
and dons purple as a sash

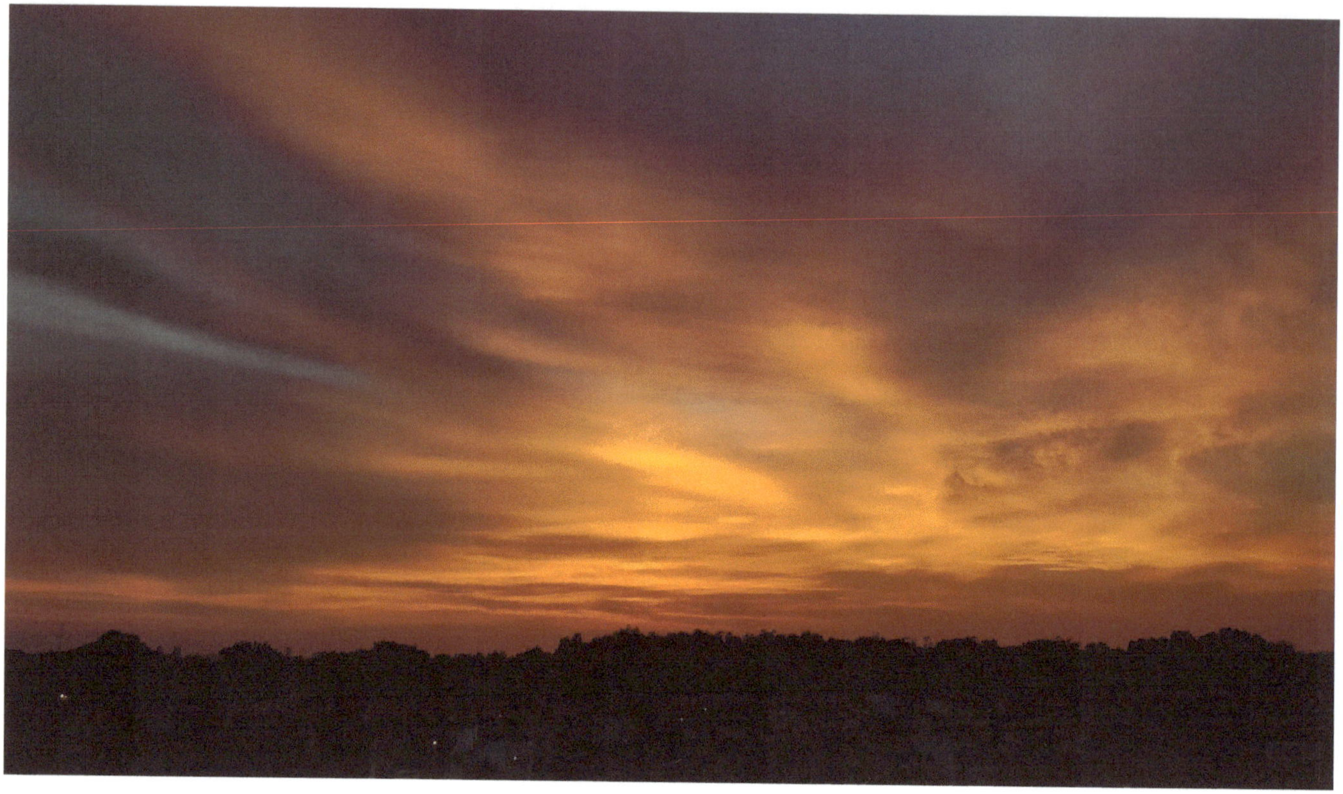

and in the end, I'll never forget
that clear skies cannot beget
the beauty that manifests
when a storm kisses a sunset

Acknowledgements

This book would not have been possible without two very special people.

Gratitude to my amazing mom, from whom I get my love for the written word. She has always been my biggest cheerleader, and her invaluable suggestions helped fine-tune the first draft of Monsoon Tales.

I also want to thank my best friend, Reena Doss, whose belief in me never waivers, who always encourages me to challenge my limits and whose loving persistence and support have made this dream of mine possible.

Best wishes,

@shrutiscapes

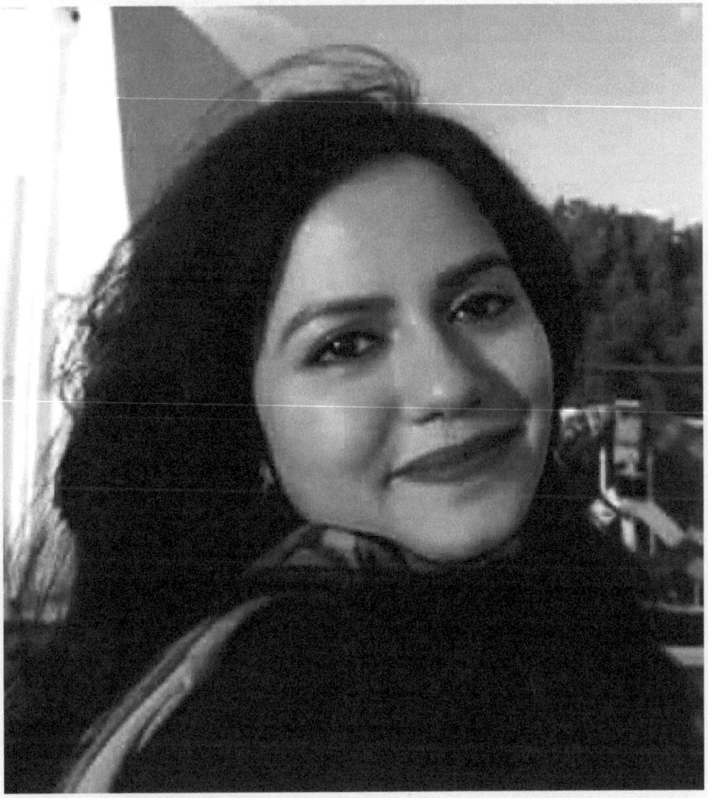

About The Author

Shruti Sharma is an introverted extrovert with a passion for all things related to travel. She prefers mountains over all other landscapes and dogs over all other animals. Her idea of a great time is to get lost in a good book, Mother Nature or with a good book in the lap of Mother Nature. Apart from her passion for photography, writing and all things blue, she loves hanging out with her family and good friends. Having left her long-time corporate job, she is currently exploring things that make her happy, publishing her work in anthologies and hoping to find her life's purpose.

Follow @shrutiscapes
Instagram | Facebook | Goodreads | Amazon
www.shrutiscapes.com

Tell Us What You Think

Write to us at contact@inkgladiatorspress.com. We might add your comments or reviews on our website as well as feature your Instagram profile. We appreciate your love for reading.

Thank you!
We remain at your service,
Reena Doss | Founder
Ink Gladiators Press®

www.ingramcontent.com/pod-product-compliance
Ingram Content Group UK Ltd.
Pitfield, Milton Keynes, MK11 3LW, UK
UKHW061433190726
13845UKWH00021B/167
* 9 7 8 9 3 9 0 7 6 6 0 9 3 *